The Emergence of Psychology as a Science

Wundt showed that **empirical methods** could be applied to mental processes. However, Watson and Skinner criticised the subjective nature of the personal observations which made it difficult to make generalisations from the research. Watson and Skinner emphasised the importance of rigorous scientific processes and carefully controlled laboratory experiments, which many psychologists still rely on today.

Cognitive psychologists believe that internal mental thoughts are an important area of study and they attempt to make inferences based on human behaviour, where they draw conclusions about cognitive processes based on human behaviour in scientific laboratory investigations.

The biological approach makes use of sophisticated technology, including brain scanning techniques, like fMRI (functional magnetic resonance imaging) and PET (positron emission tomography) scans, to understand the structure and function of the human brain. The cycle of scientific investigation is perpetuated by psychologists testing their concepts, making objective observations which can be replicated and then refining their theories according to the findings, before testing once again.

Exam Hint: For this section, it is useful to understand how each approach in psychology (those presented in the timeline above) have contributed to psychology becoming a science.

Issues and Debates

- Wundt's approach to psychological experimentation, using the method of introspection, is **idiographic** in nature. However, this was heavily criticised by the behaviourists, as universal principles that could be applied to explain human behaviour cannot be generated from introspection. Behaviourists suggest that a **nomothetic approach** to psychological investigations is more advantageous because it overcomes these limitations.

- Over the years, psychology as a discipline has become more **scientific** due to the modernisation of methods used when studying the human brain. The use of experimental methods in biological psychology, such as brain imaging techniques, demonstrate the scientific and technological advances that psychologists are now utilising.

Possible Exam Questions

1. Define what is meant by introspection. (2 marks)

2. Briefly describe the emergence of psychology as a science. (4 marks)

3. Explain Wundt's role in the development of psychology. (6 marks)

Exam Hint: Students may wish to refer to Wundt being the father of modern psychology and the origins of his investigations in Germany; explanation of his structured methods to investigate introspection and how this paved the way for later research provide suitable elaboration.

D1743432

THE BEHAVIOURIST APPROACH

Specification: Learning approaches: the behaviourist approach, including classical conditioning and Pavlov's research, operant conditioning, types of reinforcement and Skinner's research; social learning theory including imitation, identification, modelling, vicarious reinforcement, the role of mediational processes and Bandura's research.

WHAT YOU NEED TO KNOW
▪ Outline and evaluate Pavlov's classical conditioning.
▪ Outline and evaluate Skinner's operant conditioning.
▪ Outline and evaluate Bandura's social learning theory.

The Behaviourist Approach

The **behaviourist approach** is one of the most influential approaches in modern psychology. The behaviourist approach has many key assumptions, including:

1. Psychologists should only study **observable**, **quantifiable behaviour.**
2. All behaviour is **learned.**
3. Humans are no different from animals and should not be regarded as more complex.
4. Research on animal behaviour is directly relevant to humans.

Classical Conditioning

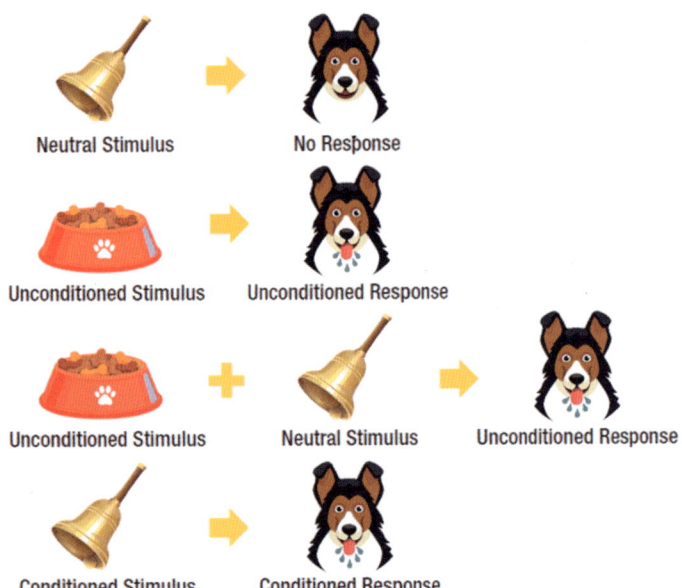

Neutral Stimulus → No Response

Unconditioned Stimulus → Unconditioned Response

Unconditioned Stimulus + Neutral Stimulus → Unconditioned Response

Conditioned Stimulus → Conditioned Response

One of the first behaviourists to explore the relationship between learning and behaviour was Ivan **Pavlov**. Pavlov developed the theory of **classical conditioning** which is a type of learning in which an existing involuntary reflex is associated with a new stimulus. He famously tested his theory using dogs, who were conditioned to **associate** the sound of a bell (**neutral stimulus**) with food (**unconditioned stimulus**). This resulted in the dogs producing a salivation response (**conditioned response**) at the sound of a bell (**conditioned stimulus**), even when no food was present. Pavlov demonstrated that repeated exposure to an event leads to a learned and uncontrollable behaviour. This process can be used to explain the acquisition of phobias and the development of attachment.

Operant Conditioning

Developing these ideas, **Skinner** suggested that behaviour is the result of learning through the consequences of our actions. Skinner conducted research into his **operant conditioning** theory using rats. He found that three **types of reinforcement** will affect behaviour:

1) **positive reinforcement** – when a behaviour is followed by a desirable consequence (reward) and is more likely to be repeated;

2) **negative reinforcement** – when a behaviour is followed by the removal of an adverse consequence and is more likely to be repeated;

3) **punishment** – when a behaviour is followed by an unpleasant consequence and is less likely to be repeated.

Exam Hint: Students often confuse negative reinforcement and punishment. Remember, negative reinforcement is the removal of an unpleasant consequent which makes a behaviour MORE likely to be repeated; whereas, punishment makes a behaviour LESS likely to be repeated.

Skinner created the Skinner box to examine operant conditioning in rats and pigeons. The animal would move around the cage, and when it pressed the lever (by accident), it would be rewarded with a food pellet. The animal would learn, through positive reinforcement, that each time it pressed the lever, it would be rewarded with food. It, therefore, learnt a new voluntary behaviour which is repeated to receive the reward again.

Evaluation of The Behaviourist Approach

- Behaviourists have significantly contributed to the still-developing recognition of **psychology as a science**. The experimental methods used by Pavlov and Skinner rejected the earlier emphasis in psychology on introspection and encouraged research that focused on more objective dimensions of behaviour. According to behaviourists, this emphasis on the scientific method has led to an increasingly valid and reliable understanding of human behaviour. These methods have also helped psychology gain credibility and status as a scientific discipline, which in turn attracts more funding and research opportunities.

- The behaviourists were influential in encouraging the use of **animals** as **research subjects**. They believed that the learning processes in humans and animals are very similar; consequently, Pavlov conducted research using dogs, and Skinner used rats and pigeons. Using non-human animals in research gives experimenters more control over the process, without demand characteristics or individual differences influencing findings. However, many consider using animals in experiments to be unethical as there is less concern about protection from harm for non-human subjects. Furthermore, some argue that findings from animal experiments are not generalisable to human behaviour: Skinner's operant conditioning theory may provide an understanding of rat behaviour, but little about human behaviour.

- The behaviourist approach has made important contributions to our modern understanding of human mental illness. For example, many phobias are thought to be the result of earlier unpleasant learning experiences. Consequently, this understanding has helped psychologists develop therapies, such as **systematic desensitisation**, that attempt to re-condition a patient's fear response. Also, some addictions such as gambling can be better understood through operant conditioning, as the rewards of gambling could be seen to reinforce the destructive behaviour. This demonstrates that the behaviourist approach has many **real-world applications** in the understanding and treatment of atypical behaviour.

- The behaviourist approach has been criticised for its limited view regarding the origins of behaviour. Behaviourists ignore alternative levels of explanation including the role of cognition and emotional factors in influencing behaviour. Skinner countered this argument, however, stating that for behaviour to be investigated scientifically, it had to be directly measurable and observable, which cognitions are not. Further to this, he said that even the most complex of human interactions could be explained using operant conditioning principles of learning by the consequences of our actions to either repeat or cease the behaviour.

Issues and Debates

- Since the behavioural approach suggests that all behaviour is learned, it falls on the **nurture** side of the **nature-nurture debate**, in which our experiences and surroundings shape our behaviour directly rather than any internal or biological factors. The behaviourist approach refers to the human mind as a **tabula rasa** (blank slate) suggesting that at birth the mind is blank and throughout life, the slate is filled while behaviour is shaped through learning.

- The fact that behaviourists believe that behaviour is controlled by something as simple as a stimulus-response association, as in classical conditioning, is an example of **environmental determinism**. Behaviourists argue that humans have little choice in their behaviour, and our behaviour is simply the product of environmental learning.

Social Learning Theory

Social learning theory (SLT) rests on the idea of **observational learning**: that learning occurs through the **observation** and **imitation** of behaviour performed by **role models,** who **model** behaviour in a social environment. Unlike the behaviourist approach, from which it derives, SLT recognises the importance of cognitive processes - mediational processes - and rejects the notion that learning is purely the outcome of a stimulus-response loop.

As its name implies, learning is a social phenomenon. In order for learning to take place, someone must model an attitude or behaviour. If the person observing the behaviour sees the person as a 'role model', they will identify with them. Identification involves associating with the qualities, characteristics and views of role models, to become more like that person. There is evidence, from Shutts et al., 2010, to suggest that for children, the age and gender similarity to models is an important determinant of imitation. This cognitive appraisal process clearly distinguishes SLT from the more deterministic behaviourist approach.

SLT is defined by four distinct mediational, or mental, processes: **attention, retention, reproduction**, and **motivation**. If these factors are implemented, imitation (i.e. copying of what has been observed) can take place; if the observed behaviour is rewarded, imitation is more likely. This learning from the observation of others is what Bandura called vicarious reinforcement.

Exam Hint: SLT is different to the other behaviourist theories, as it takes into the account the role of mediational processes (thoughts). According to Bandura, for SLT to take place, a person will form a mental representation of the behaviour and weigh up the pros and cons of being rewarded, before copying the behaviour. If the pros outweigh the cons, then they will imitate the observed behaviour.

Bandura conducted a series of experiments examining SLT as he believed that observational learning, which he called modelling, is the most important process in human learning.

Bandura, Ross & Ross (1961) – The Bobo Doll Experiment

Aim: To investigate whether aggression can be learned through social learning theory principles.

Method: 72 children (36 male and 36 female) aged between 3 and 6 years old were put into one of three groups for 10 minutes:

1) **Aggressive model** – the child played in a room while an adult hit and shouted at a "Bobo doll": a plastic inflatable toy doll which was heavy at the bottom and wobbled when hit. This group was further sub-divided by the gender of the child and the adult model, creating four conditions (see below).

2) **Non-aggressive model** – the child played in a room while an adult played quietly with a construction set. This group was further sub-divided once again by the gender of the child and the adult model, creating another four conditions (see below).

3) **Control group** – the child did not see a model.

The children were deliberately frustrated by being taken into another room where they were told that they could not play with any toys. Then, they were placed alone in a room with a range of aggressive toys (mallet, gun) and non-aggressive toys (dolls, crayons) and the Bobo doll for twenty minutes whilst being observed.

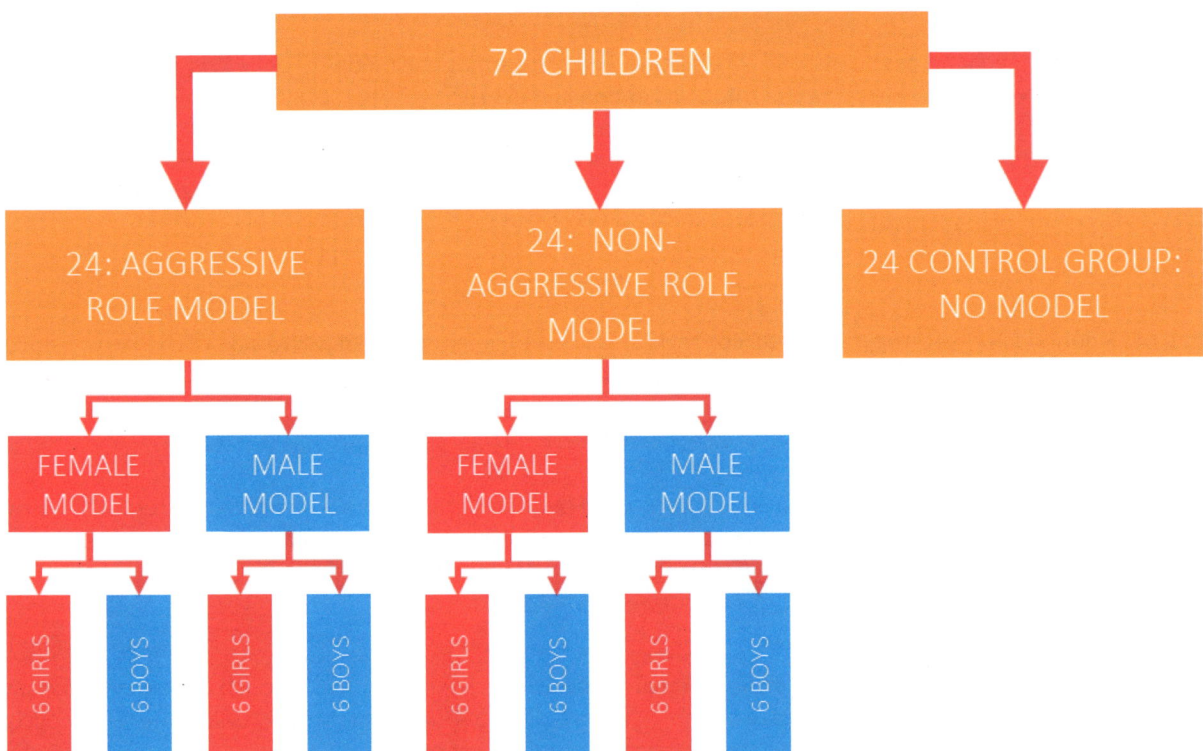

Results: Children who saw the aggressive model produced more aggressive acts than those in either of the other two groups. Boys imitated same-sex models more than girls. Girls imitated more physical aggression if they saw male models, and more verbal aggression if they saw female models.

Conclusion: Aggressive behaviour can be learned, in children, through observation and imitation of a model.

Evaluation of Social Learning Theory

- One strength of SLT is its plentiful research support. For example, **Fox and Bailenson (2009)** found that humans were more likely to imitate computer-generated 'virtual humans' who were similar to themselves; **Rushton and Campbell (1977)** found that same-sex modelling significantly increased the number of female observers who agreed to, and then actually did, donate blood; and **Myers (2015)** confirmed the importance of vicarious learning for the effectiveness of workplace teams. These studies demonstrate support for different aspects of SLT, including modelling and vicarious reinforcement, adding **credibility** to the key principles of this theory.

- The methodology used in the research to support SLT has been criticised. Bandura made extensive use of the experimental laboratory method, which is artificial, strictly-controlled and contrived in its very nature. As a result, there is the possibility of demand characteristics occurring whereby the children pick up on cues in the environment, guess the aim of the

investigation and adjust their behaviour accordingly, lowering the internal validity of the study. Therefore, the participants may have been acting in an aggressive way towards the Bobo doll because that is what they thought was expected of them rather than it being a genuine and new learned behaviour.

- A strength of SLT is its **application** to **real-world issues**. It has long been a feature in explanations of criminal behaviour (Sykes and Matza, 1957) and recent research has continued that focus (Akers, 1998). It has also been used to examine and evaluate the effectiveness of advertising: **Andsager et al. (2006)** found that 'identification with a character or example may increase the likelihood that audiences will model behaviour presented in an anti-alcohol message'. Consequently, the principles of SLT can be used to provide a positive impact on promotional health campaigns, and indirectly help combat problem behaviours like alcoholism.

- One limitation of SLT revolves around the **issue of causality**. It is not clear if people learn behaviour from models, or if they seek out models who exhibit behaviour or attitudes they already favour. **Siegel and McCormick (2006)**, for example, argue that young people who hold deviant values and attitudes are more likely to associate with similarly-inclined peers because they are more fun to be with, and thus the reinforcement of 'deviant' behaviour is a two-way process and not necessarily the result of SLT itself. Also, SLT struggles to explain complex behaviours like gender development. Children are exposed to a whole host of influences when growing up, and these different influences interact in a complex way. Consequently, it is difficult to distinguish behaviours that develop because of SLT from the many other factors that contribute to human behaviour, which poses an issue for the social learning explanation of behaviour.

Issues and Debates

- Social learning theorists recognise that behaviour is controlled by outside forces, such as modelling, but that cognitions, in the form of mediational processes, also have a role to play; as such SLT demonstrates a **soft determinism** stance.

- Bandura, in his research with the infamous Bobo doll, and later work with other researchers investigating the role of vicarious learning in shaping behaviour, take a **nomothetic approach** as he attempts to generate general laws of behaviour which can be widely applied.

Possible Exam Questions

1. A psychologist studying the role of reinforcement in shaping behaviour conducted out a laboratory experiment. To do this, she placed a rat in a box. When the rat pressed a level, first on an accidental basis, they received food treat. With each attempt thereafter, the time taken to press the lever to receive the reward decreased.

    Identify the type of conditioning being investigated in this experiment. (1 mark)

2. Briefly explain what social learning theorists mean by *modelling*. (1 mark)
Exam Hint: Although this is only a one-mark question, the response needs to provide sufficient explanation about the concept of modelling as a process whereby a person imitates the behaviour of a role model.

3. Define what social learning theorists mean by *imitation*. (1 mark)
Exam Hint: Simply offering the word 'copying' is not sufficient to gain any credit here. A sound response will explain imitation as copying behaviour of a role model. A brief example to describe imitation would also be creditworthy, but not necessary.
4. Mario often loses his temper when he becomes frustrated or angry. Most of the time he can keep his feelings under control, such as when he is at work. However, one day, after some negative feedback from his Manager, Mario stormed out of the meeting, kicking a nearby plant pot on his way so hard that it shattered.

    Suggest how a psychologist taking the behavioural approach could explain Mario's behaviour. (2 marks)
Exam Hint: Students can sometimes find it difficult to apply their knowledge and understanding of the behavioural approach to the novel scenario, in this case, Mario's behaviour. Responses must suggest how Mario would have learned the behaviours mentioned above.

5. Explain one way in which the social learning theory approach overlaps with one other approach you have studied in psychology. (2 marks)
Exam Hint: One mark is available here for identifying another suitable approach and the second mark is for explaining the overlap between the two. The most common response is likely to centre around the behaviourist approach with the common theme of all behaviour being learned. Alternatively, students may draw comparisons with the cognitive approach in psychology which highlights the role of cognitions (mediational processes) in learning.

6.   Ms Karara is a year six teacher. When it is time to go out to break or to go home, she notices that some students in her class push to the front of the queue to line up.

Explain, with reference to social learning theory, how Ms Karara might use vicarious reinforcement to modify the behaviour of her students. (3 marks)

Exam Hint: To demonstrate sound knowledge and understanding of the concept of vicarious reinforcement, candidates must include reference to the fact that the students will need to observe a model being reinforced (rewarded by Ms Karara) for appropriate behaviour (lining up without pushing in) whilst linking it closely to the scenario.

7.   Describe one procedure that behavioural psychologists have used to investigate conditioning. (3 marks)

Exam Hint: It is crucial for responses to this question to focus on the procedural elements and not the findings or conclusions drawn. Reference to a controlled environment, association forming between a stimulus and a response (Pavlov), and/or any rewards given (Skinner) which perpetuates the behaviour are suitable here.

8.   Debbie is telling a story of her childhood to her friend, Harj: "When I was six, and at my sisters' birthday party, a balloon burst near my face with a really loud bang. Even to this day, balloons still terrify me and I cannot go near them!"

Using your knowledge and understanding of classical conditioning, explain why Debbie is scared by balloons. (3 marks)

Exam Hint: Students must apply their knowledge of classical conditioning accurately to the scenario with Debbie and balloons using the key terms associated with classical conditioning: NS, UCS, UCR, CS and CR.

9.   Heather has just started learning to ice skate and is keen to skate well. She watches other skaters on the ice carefully. When she sees another skater make a difficult turn, she then tries to copy the same move. She considers how the other skater was positioning their body weight on their ice blades and whether she can do the same.

Mediational processes have a central role to play in social learning theory. With reference to Heather's experience, outline the role of mediational processes in social learning. (4 marks)

10.   Identify and explain two strengths of the behaviourist approach in psychology. (4 marks)

Exam Hint: Students can sometimes find it difficult to express the strengths of the behavioural approach in psychology clearly. Unfortunately, points often identified as strengths are merely features of the approach and, as such, answers describe Pavlov or Skinner's work with no link why this is a strength. Sound answers are likely to focus on the use of experimental methodology and the scientific nature of the approach.

11.   A psychology A-level student, Sian, went home and was telling her Dad, Dafydd, about what she had learned at college that day:

Sian said: "The behaviourist approach has been really influential in understanding human behaviour.
But, so much of the research has been conducted using animals as participants.' Discuss the value of the behaviourist approach in understanding human behaviour. (5 marks)

Exam Hint: To gain full credit for this question, students must sustain a discussion on the value of the behaviourist approach rather than going into great depth with the outline of the main assumptions. The most likely discussion will come from the advantages and disadvantages of research using animals and generalising findings to human behaviour, given the scenario provided about Sian's discussion with her Dad.

12.   Kym got trapped in a lift for several hours when it broke down. Now, she cannot face going into a lift at all and is filled with fear at the very thought.

Joshua is given some chocolate for cleaning out the litter tray for their pet cat. Jermaine, his twin brother, saw this. The next day, the twin's mum finds Jermaine cleaning out the cat's litter tray.

Describe how the behaviour of Kym and Jermaine can be explained by the learning approach in psychology. (6 marks)

Exam Hint: To score well on this question, students must have sound knowledge and understanding of both classical conditioning and social learning theory and the ability to effectively apply the main features to the cases of Kym and Jermaine, using the material provided in the scenario.

13.   A behavioural psychologist conducted a study investigating the phenomena of social learning. Within the procedure, they showed young children a film of a similarly-aged infant stroking a kitten. Whilst the participants were viewing the film, the psychologist made verbal comments on how kind the child on the screen was for petting the animal so gently. After the film had finished, the psychologist brought a real kitten into the room to observe how the participants behaved.

Explain what is meant by the social learning theory approach and explain how social learning may have occurred due to the procedure the behaviourist psychologist used in their investigation. (6 marks)

14. Discuss two limitations of social learning theory. (6 marks)

15. Outline and evaluate the behaviourist approach in psychology. (12/16 marks)

16. Discuss the social learning theory approach in psychology. (12/16 marks)

17. Outline and evaluate the influence of behaviourists, such as Pavlov and Skinner, to psychologists' understanding of human behaviour. (12/16 marks)

18. Discuss social learning theory. In your answer, draw comparisons to at least one other approach you have studied in psychology. (16 marks)

Exam Hint: If comparisons are made to other approaches, such as behavioural or cognitive, during the evaluative discussion, students must make sure that they align their response with why this is a strength or a limitation of the social learning theory.

THE COGNITIVE APPROACH

Specification: The study of internal mental processes, the role of schema, the use of theoretical and computer models to explain and make inferences about mental processes. The emergence of cognitive neuroscience.

WHAT YOU NEED TO KNOW
▪ Outline and evaluate the cognitive approach.

The cognitive approach focuses on the examination of **internal mental processes** such as perception, memory, attention and consciousness. Since these processes are internal and cannot be studied directly, their operation must be inferred from the observation and measurement of visible human behaviour.

To assist this **inference**, cognitive psychologists make use of **theoretical models** and **computer models.** Theoretical models enable the visual representation of complex conceptual processes, and computer models provide a basis for research within the field of cognitive psychology.

The Study of Internal Mental Processes

Internal mental processes are the operations that occur during thinking. Examples include how we turn the information from our eyes into a usable form (**perception**); how we choose what to think about (**attention**); how we store information to use in the future (**memory**); how we construct meaningful sentences to communicate with others (**language**); and how we construct new solutions (**problem-solving**). Cognitive psychologists appreciate that these concepts cannot be directly observed and use **inferences** as a means of understanding human experience from observable behaviours.

The Role of The Schema

Schema theory is an information-processing model that emphasises how perception and memory are shaped by cognitive frameworks. Schemas are mental frameworks of information that we use to organise past experiences and to interpret and respond to new situations. For example, a classroom schema might consist of a whiteboard, tables, chairs, books, pens and a teacher. As we age, our schemas become increasingly sophisticated, and adults develop more and more schemas to cover most situations.

Schemas are an example of **top-down information-processing,** because they provide us with expectations about what will happen in the world, rather than requiring us to process every single detail, all of the time. Schemas allow us to make sense of ambiguous situations by "filling in the gaps" in our knowledge. They enable us to act comfortably even when our information is incomplete which makes it much easier to deal with complex situations. However, schemas can lead to errors in information-processing such as prejudice and discrimination.

The Use of Theoretical Models

Theoretical models are visual representations of internal mental processes that are used to help researchers simplify and study complex processes. Theoretical models are typically diagrams or flowcharts that show how information is passed between the different systems that manipulate it. For example, the multi-store model **(Atkinson and Shiffrin, 1968)** is a theoretical model of memory. Likewise, the working memory model **(Baddeley and Hitch, 1974)** is a theoretical model of short-term memory.

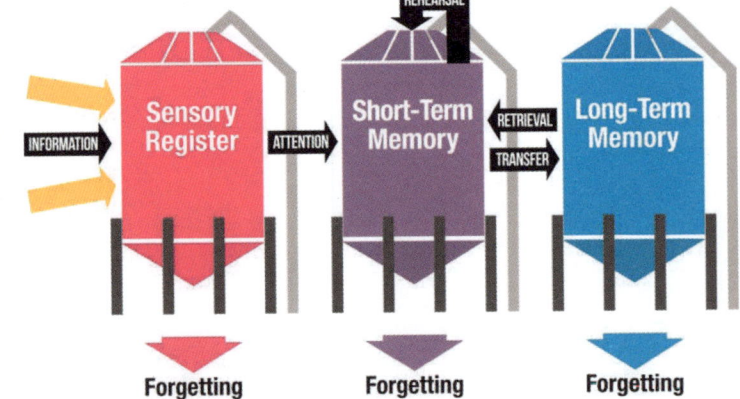

The Use of Computer Models

The development of the computer in the 1960s led to computer models emerging within psychology to explain different mental processes. For example, the analogy of long-term memory being the hard disk and short-term (working memory) being viewed as the computer's RAM (Random Access Memory) has been applied to the human brain. Computer models of memory have been particularly useful in the development of artificial intelligence (AI).

The Emergence of Cognitive Neuroscience

Cognitive neuroscience is a relatively new field that tries to bridge the gap between the cognitive and biological approaches. This field has resulted from the development of techniques for scanning the living brain while it is actively processing information. Cognitive neuroscience uses non-invasive brain scanning techniques like PET (positron emission tomography) scans and MRIs (magnetic resonance imaging) to understand which parts of the brain are active while specific internal mental processes are being used.

For example, brain scans have highlighted the distinction between different types of long-term memory (LTM). The **hippocampus** is associated with **episodic memory**; the **temporal lobe** is associated with **semantic memory,** and the **cerebellum** and **motor cortex** are associated with **procedural memories.** Brain imaging techniques have also been successful in establishing a link to certain mental health disorders, such as the association between obsessive compulsive disorder (OCD) and the **parahippocampal gyrus**.

Evaluation of The Cognitive Approach

- Recent advances in neuroimaging technology, such as fMRI (functional magnetic resonance imaging), have lent weight to theoretical models by providing empirical confirmation of brain activity for specific cognitive functions under controlled conditions. However, the precise meaning of this activity is still a matter for debate. Some claim that these techniques provide the cognitive approach with a strong scientific grounding, while others insist that neuroimaging evidence is only correlational, and therefore does not constitute true scientific validation of either theories or models. Nevertheless, the availability of such techniques and their increasing sophistication is one clear strength of the cognitive approach.

- A speciality of the cognitive approach is its recognition of the complexity of human behaviour, and thus its hesitation to assert a reductionist explanation of mental processes. There can be no doubt that all cognition rests on a biological foundation since it occurs in the brain and is made possible by its operation. But the precise nature of consciousness and memory and perception are not easily reducible to purely biological outcomes, as the lived experience of all human beings seems to demonstrate consistently.

- The cognitive approach has many real-world applications. For example, cognitive research into memory and the effects of misleading information has reduced the use of eyewitness testimony in court cases, and led to major reforms in police procedure, like the use of the cognitive interview. Additionally, a better understanding of thinking patterns has helped professionals understand and treat mental illnesses such as depression through the use of therapies like CBT. This indicates that cognitive research has made concrete contributions to contemporary society and has developed professional understanding in many fields.

- However, not all human behaviour can be captured under the cognitive umbrella; the research in this field has tended to neglect other significant dimensions of behaviour such as emotion and motivation which may be linked to cognition, but are not the same. The cognitive approach is careful to insist that we are more than biological machines but often overlooks the equally important fact that we are not only cognitive creatures.

Issues and Debates

- The cognitive approach pays respect to both the **nature and nurture** element of this debate. It recognises that behaviour is the result of information processing which occurs in the brain and is of biological origin (nature), while concepts such as schema are modified by experience in the environment (nurture).

- Furthermore, the cognitive approach straddles both the **nomothetic and idiographic** approaches in psychology since it utilises both experimental methods to generate universal laws to explain behaviour and draws on the findings of individual case studies, such as Phineas Gage and Clive Wearing (see the Memory Topic Companion).

Possible Exam Questions

1. Explain what is meant by 'inference'. (1 mark)
Exam Hint: Although this is only a one-mark question, responses must provide an accurate and detailed explanation of inference. For example, inference means to make assumptions about internal mental processes that cannot be observed directly.

2. Outline **one** issues with studying internal mental processes. (2 marks)
Exam Hint: A likely issue that students will present is that the direct observation of the processes involved in human memory is not possible. As a result, inferences are made from the observable behaviour of participants. This process, however, could be incorrect or subject to experimenter bias.

3. Explain **one** strength and **one** limitation of the cognitive approach. (4 marks)
Exam Hint: It is important for students to read the question carefully and only explain one strength and one limitation rather than presenting a rote-learned evaluation response for this approach. A likely strength which could be explained is the use of

theoretical or computer models for ease of understanding. A common limitation is that inferences about cognitive processes are required since they cannot be observed directly.

4.   Identify **two** main assumptions of the cognitive approach in psychology. For **each** assumption, justify your response with reference to a topic in psychology. (4 marks)

Exam Hint: In order for students to gain full credit for this question, they must ensure that their chosen applications to topics in psychology are not vague and are fully elaborated. Likely options for the application are to depression and memory although other areas are equally creditworthy if justified well.

5.   Outline **two** features of the cognitive approach. Explain **two** limitations of the cognitive approach. (8 marks)

Exam Hint: The downfall of most students attempting this sort of question is achieving success in the second part which requires evaluation. It is important for answers to present a clear and coherent line of argument to provide a well-elaborated discussion about the limitations of the cognitive approach in psychology. Focusing heavily on providing more description in the absence of any evaluation will not earn any more credit regardless of how accurate it is.

6.   Discuss the cognitive approach in psychology. (12/16 marks)

7.   Outline the cognitive approach. Evaluate the research methods used by cognitive psychologists in this field of investigation. (16 marks)

Exam Hint: For this question, it is important that students can draw upon their research methods knowledge and understanding to evaluate the cognitive approach with reference, for example, to laboratory experiments and case studies.

8.   Outline key assumptions of the cognitive approach. Compare the cognitive approach in psychology with the psychodynamic approach. (16 marks)

Exam Hint: This question is only relevant to students undertaking the full A-level route since comparison of approaches is not part of the AS level specification. Students must take their time to carefully read the question and plan their answer strategically to meet the demands of the question which requires direct comparisons of the two approaches, not isolated evaluation points of the cognitive or psychodynamic approaches.

THE BIOLOGICAL APPROACH

Specification: The influence of genes, biological structures and neurochemistry on behaviour. Genotype and phenotype, genetic basis of behaviour, evolution and behaviour.

WHAT YOU NEED TO KNOW
▪ Outline and evaluate the biological approach.

The biological approach assumes that all human behaviour has a biological origin. This approach insists that to comprehend human behaviour fully, it is necessary to understand internal **biological structures** and processes including **genes**, the nervous system, and **neurochemistry**.

The Influence of Genes: Genotype and Phenotype

Genes are passed on from one generation to the next. Genes carry information in the form of DNA, which carry instructions for characteristics, such as eye colour, intelligence, etc. A person's **genotype** is their genetic makeup, which is fixed from birth. A person's **phenotype** is the expression of their genes which leads to the observable characteristics of a person. The phenotype is influenced by both the genetic inheritance and the interaction of this with the environment.

Geneticists working within this approach have found evidence that some behavioural or psychological characteristics, such as intelligence or psychological illness, can be inherited in a similar way to physical characteristics, such as eye and hair colour. Much research in this area has used **monozygotic** (MZ) twins because they share 100% of their DNA (often called identical twins) in comparison to **dizygotic** (DZ) twins (non-identical) who share 50% of their DNA.

For example, recent research has found that MZ twins have an increased **concordance rate** of developing schizophrenia compared to DZ twins. Other psychological conditions are also influenced by genes. For example, **McGuffin et al. (1996)** found that if one identical twin has depression, there is a **46%** chance that the other twin will also have depression. This suggests that there is a genetic component to illnesses like schizophrenia and depression. These relationships are important for understanding the genetic component of psychological illnesses and demonstrate the impact of genes on certain human conditions.

The Influence of Biological Structures

Biological psychologists believe that the structure of organs, such as the brain, central nervous system (CNS), the peripheral nervous system (PNS) and the endocrine system determine our behaviour. The nervous system transmits messages through a type of nerve cell called a neuron. Many examples of human behaviour are controlled by neuronal action including eating (feeling hungry and satiated) and breathing. Furthermore, research has shown that the different lobes of the brain are linked with general functions, for example, the **occipital lobe** is associated with visual perception, and the **parietal lobe** is linked to the processing of sensory information.

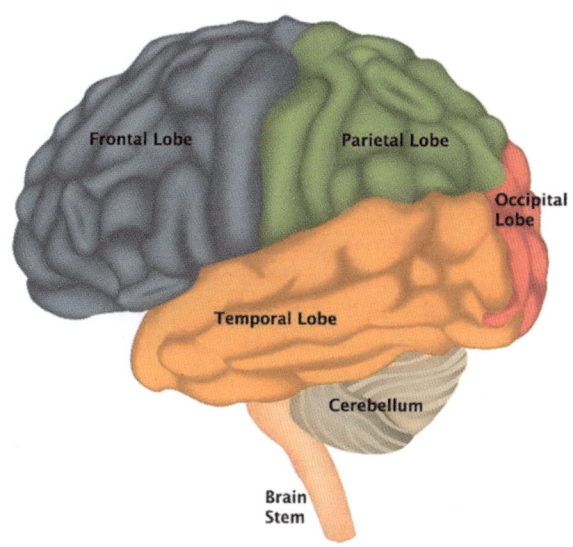

The effect of damage to the brain is demonstrated by the case study of **Phineas Gage** who lost his ability to inhibit antisocial behaviour after an explosion sent an iron bar through his head, destroying a large portion of his **frontal cortex.** This case study demonstrates the influence of a biological structure (frontal cortex) on behaviour (inhibition).

The Influence of Neurochemistry

Biological psychologists also recognise the role of chemicals in determining behaviour. At the synapse, signals are sent between neurones by chemicals called neurotransmitters. Imbalances in the number of neurotransmitters are associated with atypical behaviour, for example, too little **serotonin** has been associated with depression and too much **dopamine** has been associated with schizophrenia.

Research in this area helps us to understand the role of neurotransmitters. For example, recent research suggests that abnormally low levels of serotonin are linked to aggressive behaviour, indicating that this neurotransmitter is important in regulating behaviour and impulse control (**Crockett et al., 2008**).

Other types of chemicals found in the body which can also influence behaviour are called **hormones.** They are released into the bloodstream where they travel to the target cells which are activated by them specifically. **Carre et al., (2006)** found that high levels of testosterone are associated with defensiveness and territoriality in a study investigating the behaviour of ice hockey players.

Evolution and Behaviour

Genes are the mechanism through which evolution takes place. The process of **natural selection**, proposed by Darwin, ensures that characteristics which provide an evolutionary advantage, such as survival and enhanced reproductive chances, are passed from one generation to the next, whilst others which do not, die out.

A classic example of evolutionary psychology research is **Buss's (1994)** survey of heterosexual mate selection. Across all 37 countries studied, he found that men preferred good looks, youth and chastity, while women preferred good financial prospects, industriousness and dependability. These results suggest that certain behaviours and traits have evolved in both males and females since they promote better prospects for passing on favourable genes.

Evaluation of The Biological Approach

- One limitation of the biological approach is that **causation** is often strongly implied in explanations that focus on brain structures. For example, one explanation of schizophrenia suggests that a lack of activity in the ventral striatum is linked to the development of negative symptoms such as avolition. This is a problem for biological explanations because such research tells us only that there is an association between brain structures and behaviour; it cannot tell us that the reduced activity in that area of the brain causes the behaviour, or that the behaviour causes lower activity in that part of the brain. Therefore, it is critically important to remember that biological explanations are often based on correlational results, which does not mean that one event causes the other.

- Another weakness of this approach is that biological explanations of human behaviour may be considered **deterministic**. For example, one assumption of the biological approach is that some human behaviours are the result of evolution: they maximise our chances of survival and reproduction and thus are 'naturally selected' and inherited from our ancestors. Such evolutionary claims are used to explain a variety of gender differences in human behaviour including aggression and stress. Such explanations imply that humans have little control over their behaviour, and suggest we are predetermined to act in a certain way regardless of experience, free will, or the environment. This is problematic for those who do not follow 'typical' or 'expected' behaviours and overemphasises the role of nature on behaviour. It is also an explanation that is unfalsifiable, and thus incapable of scientific validation.

- However, a strength of the biological approach is that it often utilises **reliable** methods of research. For example, some research into genetics and neurochemistry requires precise scientific methodology, such as **fMRIs, PET scans, drug trials, and EEGs**. These techniques provide psychologists with an accurate measure of internal processes that were previously not accessible. This makes biological evidence less susceptible to misinterpretation or **experimenter bias** which is a strength of such research.

- Another strength of the biological approach is that it has many **real-world applications**. Drug therapies have been developed for many mental illnesses based on research into neurotransmitters; antidepressants work to increase serotonin levels in the brain, based on the understanding of how low levels of serotonin contribute to depressive symptoms. Understanding 'abnormal' neurochemical activity in the brain has not only been helpful for developing treatments but has also provided patients with an explanation that their illness is not their fault.

Issues and Debates

- In order for complex human behaviour to be analysed and best understood, according to biological psychologists, it must be broken down into its component parts. This means that phenomena are explained using genetic, neurochemical or structural explanations resulting in the biological approach taking a **reductionist (biological)** perspective.

- Whilst it is widely accepted that the biological approach takes the **nature** side of the nature-nurture debate, since behaviour is determined by innate features including genes and neurotransmitters, acknowledgement is paid to the role of the environment with the interaction of the two influencing an individual's phenotype.

Possible Exam Questions

1. Identify which of the following describes a **phenotype**. Shade one box only. (1 mark)
   A. The influence of genotype and evolution.
   B. The impact of genetic makeup intertwined with neurotransmitters.
   C. An interaction between inheritance and the environment.
   D. A combination of neurotransmitters and environment.

2. Identify which **one** of the following statements about evolution is **incorrect** by shading **one** box only. (1 mark)
   A. Evolution involves those humans best suited for survival breeding together.
   B. The process of evolution involves adaptation.
   C. Through evolution, behaviour is changed from one generation to the next.
   D. Evolution suggests that species have genetic material in common.

3. Explain what is meant by the term evolution with reference to human behaviour. You may provide an example to support your answer. (3 marks)

4. Briefly describe the influence of genes on behaviour. (3 marks)

5. Using an example to illustrate your point, explain the difference between genotype and phenotype. (3 marks)

6. Define what is meant by *genotype* and *phenotype*. Provide an example for each. (4 marks)
Exam Hint: Genotype refers to the genetic make-up of an individual and phenotype is the expression of genes which results in the observable characteristics of a person. The latter is influenced by both the genetic inheritance and interaction with the environment and must be present in the response for full credit to be awarded.

7. Monozygotic (identical) twins, Ikhlas and Vinay, were separated at birth. On their fortieth birthday, they finally met up with one another. Whilst they were talking, they realised that they had very different personality traits: Ikhlas is very sociable whereas Vinay is more introverted.

   Using your knowledge and understanding of genotype and phenotype, explain the personality differences of Ikhlas and Vinay. (4 marks)
Exam Hint: Successful answers for this question will demonstrate a sound knowledge of genotype and phenotype whilst engaging fully with the scenario provided. For example, for Ikhlas and Vinay to have developed different personality traits (sociable/introverted), their genotype (genetic inheritance) must have interacted with their differing environments during their separate upbringing to produce the differences observed (phenotype)

8. Explain the influence of biological structures on human behaviour. (4 marks)

9. Explain **one** strength and **one** limitation of the biological approach in psychology. (6 marks)

10. Discuss the biological approach in psychology. (12/16 marks)

11. Discuss the biological approach to explaining human behaviour. Include at least **one** comparison to another approach in psychology in your response. (16 marks)

THE PSYCHODYNAMIC APPROACH [A-LEVEL ONLY]

The psychodynamic approach: the role of the unconscious, the structure of personality, that is ID, ego and superego, defence mechanisms including repression, denial and displacement, psychosexual stages.

WHAT YOU NEED TO KNOW
▪ Outline and evaluate the psychodynamic approach.

The foundations of the **psychodynamic approach** were laid by **Sigmund Freud**. He proposed the notion of the **unconscious**, which lies at the root of his hugely influential theory. Central to the psychodynamic approach are three main assumptions: **personality** (psyche) has a discernible structure (**ID, ego** and **superego**); that it is constructed by the passage through **psychosexual stages** of development throughout infancy and adolescence; and that the unconscious conflicts in the psyche are mediated by processes called **defence mechanisms.**

The Role of The Unconscious

According to the psychodynamic approach, there are vast parts of the mind that are inaccessible to conscious awareness. The metaphor of an iceberg was used by Freud to explain this, with consciousness being the small part of the structure which we are aware of (the top of the iceberg), and the unconscious taking up a much larger proportion of the human mind (beneath the surface), even though we are not directly aware or able to access it at will.

Any traumatic events or memories from childhood are repressed into the unconscious mind and kept there, hidden from conscious awareness. However, psychodynamic theorists suggest that such events or memories are never truly forgotten and can be explored through psychoanalysis.

The unconscious mind can reveal itself in several ways including dreams, fantasies and slips of the tongue, otherwise known as 'Freudian slips'.

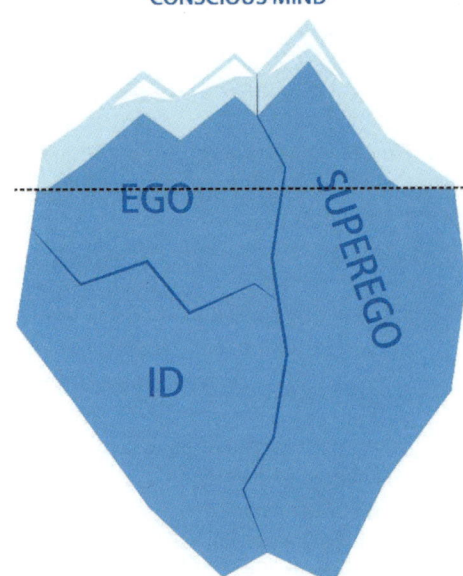

CONSCIOUS MIND

UNCONSCIOUS MIND

The Structure of The Personality: ID, Ego and Superego

According to Freud, the personality is made up of three components: the ID, ego and superego.

1. The **ID** is pure erotic energy and is governed by the pleasure principle. It consists of primal urges which Freud called drives and seeks nothing but pleasure and instant gratification. It operates on instinct and is the part of the personality which is present at birth.

2. The **ego** is governed by the reality principle and is tasked with taming the id and balancing the demands of the superego, much like a referee overseeing a football match. The ego is not present at birth and arises in response to control by others, specifically parents during the anal stage of development (see below), at around two years old.

3. The **superego** is governed by the morality principal: our sense of right and wrong. It is characterised by the 'inner voice' that tells us when we have crossed into the boundaries of unacceptable behaviour. The superego is the internalised parent and develops in response to parental discipline around five years old.

Defence Mechanisms

Defence mechanisms are used by the ego in order to cope with the conflicting demands of the other two parts of the personality: the ID and superego. The ego works by distorting reality so that the individual can continue with their everyday life without unpleasant feelings or memories dominating their conscious awareness.

DEFENCE MECHANISM	EXPLANATION	EXAMPLE
REPRESSION	Repression occurs when a traumatic or distressing memory is forced out of conscious awareness and into the unconscious mind.	An adult who experienced neglect at the hands of their parents as a child may have no conscious awareness that this trauma occurred, although they may show distrust of others in later life.
DENIAL	Denial involves a refusal to accept the truth or reality of a situation, acting as though nothing distressing has happened.	Someone with a gambling addiction may deny that they have a problem with their finances despite being in a large amount of debt.
DISPLACEMENT	Displacement is when the feelings towards a target individual cannot be expressed directly and are therefore transferred onto someone/something else.	Someone who was bullied at school may go home and take it out by being mean towards their younger sibling.

Psychosexual Stages

According to Freud, children pass through several psychosexual stages of development: **oral, anal, phallic, latent** and **genital**. During each stage, the child has its desires for bodily pleasure denied and redirected by its parents until they focus exclusively on the appropriate sexual outlet for the given stage. According to Freud, if a child fails to resolve the conflict at each of the psychosexual stages, they may develop a fixation where they display certain behaviours/characteristics in their adult life.

The driver of this process is the **Oedipus complex** in which boys relinquish their unconscious desire for their mother and internalise the fear of castration by their father. This process is traumatic, and cannot be confronted directly, and so the ego establishes defence mechanisms, such as repression and denial, to mediate the psychological terrors it generates.

STAGE	AGE	FOCUS	DESCRIPTION	UNRESOLVED CONFLICT / FIXATION
ORAL	0-2	Mouth	The infant experiences pleasure through their mouth, particularly sucking and biting.	Oral fixation: here a person might engage in behaviours like smoking, nail-biting, etc.
ANAL	2-3	Anus	The child becomes aware of the reality principle imposed by the parents and must undergo potty training in order to control their bowel movements. It is during this stage the Ego develops.	Anal fixation can manifest in two ways. 1) Anal retentive: here a person might become an obsessive perfectionist; 2) Anal explusive: here a person might be messy and thoughtless.
PHALLIC	3-6	Genitals	The major feature of this stage is the Oedipus complex in which infant boys must overcome their unconscious sexual desire for their mother by identifying with their father. It is during this stage that the Superego develops.	A phallic fixation or phallic personal might manifest in reckless and narcissistic behaviours.
LATENT	6-puberty	Hidden	The sexual energy which has driven the previous stages now becomes latent, so the individual can focus on the world around them and form friendships.	N/A.
GENITAL	Puberty +	Forming heterosexual relationships	The final stage culminates with the psychosexual energy taking residence in the genitals, to be directed towards the formation of adult relationships.	A person who becomes fixated at the genital stage might struggle to form heterosexual relationships.

Exam Hint: The mnemonic Old Age Pensioners Like Grapes may help you to remember the correct sequence of the psychosexual stages.

Evaluation of The Psychodynamic Approach

- As strange as Freud's ideas may seem now, they have been enormously influential in both the practice of psychology and in our understanding of how culture operates. The evidence for these ideas is almost entirely clinical rather than empirical, and its scientific credibility is questionable. But few would deny that there are, in fact, unconscious motives and demonstrable defence mechanisms. These existential realities have allowed Freudian theory to maintain some hold on psychotherapeutic techniques, like psychoanalysis, which is still used to treat patients with deep-seated psychological health issues today.

- There is empirical research to support the effectiveness of psychoanalysis. **Biskup et al., (2005)** reported a naturalistic study of 36 patients that demonstrated that at the end of psychoanalytic therapy, 77% of the patients showed clinically significant improvements. Furthermore, **Bachrach et al., (2000)** conducted a meta-analysis of every major study of the effectiveness of psychoanalytic treatment and found that all the studies show that psychoanalysis is an effective treatment for many patients. This suggests that despite a lack of empirical support for psychodynamic theories psychodynamic treatments (e.g. psychoanalysis) are effective at treating a range of psychological disorders.

- Freud's ideas demonstrate a significant gender bias; his obsession with the Oedipus complex is intensely **androcentric**, and many would claim this makes them irrelevant to an understanding of women. But female psychoanalysts like **Melanie Klein** have shown that even gender-biased theories can be adapted to provide useful insights into female behaviour. Therefore, while Freud's original ideas demonstrate a significant gender bias, his work has been used to develop important and influential theories that apply to women.

- Psychoanalytic theory has been criticised for being **culturally biased**. All of Freud's patients came from the Viennese middle-class, and his universal generalisations were based on this highly unrepresentative sample. He called his therapy "the talking cure", and there is considerable evidence to suggest that it is only suitable for cultures where the discussion of personal problems is encouraged. This is more a practical limitation than a conceptual one, but it casts some doubt on the effectiveness of any therapeutic approach, for other cultures, based on psychoanalytic ideas.

Issues and Debates

- The psychodynamic approach suggests that human behaviour is governed by unconscious drives and early traumatic childhood experiences which are repressed into the unconscious mind. As such, an individual does not have free will over their behaviour and instead is under the influence of **psychic determinism**.

- A major criticism of Freudian theory is that it is not empirically testable. For example, the human mind cannot be dissected to reveal the id, ego and superego. As a result, it is **not scientific** in its approach to explaining human behaviour since the understanding of behaviour relies solely on the subjective interpretation of the psychoanalyst.

Possible Exam Questions

1. Identify which of the following statements about *repression* is **false**. Only shade **one** box.   (1 mark)
   A. It causes trouble for individuals trying to access unpleasant recollections.
   B. It can lead to unpleasant memories causing psychological suffering.
   C. It involves unpleasant recollections being kept in the unconscious mind.
   D. It involves individuals choosing to forget unpleasant events.

2. Identify which of the following statements is **false**. Only shade **one** box. (1 mark)
   a) The ID is selfish.
   b) The ID needs instant gratification.
   c) The Superego is responsible for a person's sense of right and wrong.
   d) The Superego is responsible for unacceptable behaviours.

3. Mario often loses his temper when he becomes frustrated or angry. Most of the time he can keep his feelings under control, such as when he is at work. However, one day, after some negative feedback from his Manager, Mario stormed out of the meeting, kicking a nearby plant pot on his way so hard that it shattered.

   Suggest how a psychodynamic psychologist could explain Mario's behaviour. (2 marks)

   Exam Hint: Students can sometimes find it difficult to apply their knowledge and understanding of the psychodynamic approach to a novel scenario, in this case, Mario's behaviour. Responses might suggest how Mario's behaviour could be governed by the defence mechanism of displacement since he cannot take out his anger on this Manager directly he opts to direct it towards the pot plant.

4. A psychologist following the psychodynamic approach within psychology was interested in investigating the purpose of dreams. To do this, she asked four of her friends to write a journal each morning about the dreams they had the

previous night, for seven consecutive days. The psychologist then set about analysing the content of the dream journals based on the assumption that they contained repressed desires.

With reference to the scenario above, explain why psychologists following the psychodynamic approach in psychology have been heavily criticised for disregarding scientific principles. (3 marks)

Exam Hint: To gain full credit here, students must present sound knowledge and understanding of the psychodynamic approach, scientific principles and relate it appropriately to the scenario. Without linking the concepts, such as a lack of objectivity, to the scenario outlining dream journals, no marks will be awarded. To avoid this pitfall, students need to read the question carefully to fulfil the demands carefully.

5. Explain **one** limitation of the psychodynamic approach in psychology. (2 marks)

Exam Hint: It is important that students only present one limitation with elaboration rather than two in less detail to fulfil the requirements of this question fully.

6. Loren was very keen to pass her driving test so she could have the freedom to visit her friends whenever she wanted to. After her test, which she failed, she did not seem disappointed or upset.

Identify **one** defence mechanism and explain why Loren was not upset after failing her driving test. (2 marks)

Exam Hint: Most students are likely to identify denial as an appropriate defence mechanism for the case of Loren since she appears to be refusing to accept the reality of her situation, acting as though nothing disappointing has happened.

7. Elise is out shopping and sees a bracelet that she thinks is perfect for her upcoming night out. She notices that there are no security guards or cameras and considers how easy it would be for her to take it without paying by slipping it into her handbag.

Describe the psychodynamic explanation for the development of the superego component of the personality (psyche). Explain how the superego might influence moral behaviour in Elise's situation. (4 marks)

Exam Hint: Students must ensure that their description of the psychodynamic theory of personality development, specifically the superego, is tied to their explanation of moral development. The scenario with Elise should provide help with this as most students will be able to identify the unconscious internal conflict Elise must have been experiencing.

8. Outline and evaluate the psychodynamic approach in psychology, including at least **one** difference between the psychodynamic approach and the humanistic approach in your response. (8 marks)

Exam Hint: A possible comparison presented in response to this questions could include the difference in assumptions between the two approaches with psychodynamic psychologists believing that repressed memories influence human behaviour whereas he humanistic approach believes in the power of the present for personal growth to occur for the individual. Alternatively, students may refer to the different approaches to treatment.

9. Discuss the psychodynamic approach in psychology. (16 marks)

10. Outline the cognitive approach. Compare the cognitive approach with the psychodynamic approach in psychology. (16 marks)

Exam Hint: With questions such as this, the evaluation marks available can only be earned by making points which directly compare the two approaches named – cognitive and psychodynamic. General evaluation commentary relating to the cognitive approach is not creditworthy. Students must, therefore, read the question carefully before planning their response to meet the demands of the question.

11. Discuss the unique nature of the psychodynamic approach. In your answer, you must refer to other approaches in psychology. (16 marks)

Exam Hint: In instances such as this, a pre-prepared essay on the psychodynamic approach will not address the needs of this question which is asking for the response to be tailored towards why the approach is unique. Careful consideration needs to be given to the points which will be discussed in the content of the essay before the student begins to write so that a clear and coherent response is developed.

12. Discuss the psychodynamic approach to explaining human behaviour. The evaluation must refer to both strengths **and** limitations of the approach. (16 marks)

Exam Hint: It is important to note that comparisons with other approaches will only be credited for this question if the response makes it clear how the value of the psychodynamic approach is weakened as a result. Likely evaluation points might include the development of talking therapy (strength) and the central concepts, such as the unconscious mind, not being scientifically testable (limitation).

HUMANISTIC PSYCHOLOGY [A-LEVEL ONLY]

Specification: Humanistic psychology: free will, self-actualisation and Maslow's hierarchy of needs, focus on the self, congruence, the role of conditions of worth. The influence on counselling psychology.

WHAT YOU NEED TO KNOW
▪ Outline and evaluate the humanistic approach.

There are many strands of **humanistic psychology**, but all draw on the work of the field's founding figures, **Abraham Maslow** and **Carl Rogers**. Humanistic psychology is different from the other approaches in psychology as it is intensively focused on discovering what it means to be fully human. Humanistic psychologists insist that the other approaches in psychology are reductionist, deterministic and, as a result, cannot explain the holistic complexity of human behaviour.

Free Will

Humanistic psychology assumes that every individual can assert **free will** and have a choice in how they behave. This means that everyone can consciously control and influence their own personal destiny, even within the constraints that exist in life from outside forces. This idea makes the humanistic approach radically different from the other approaches that suggest that human behaviour is, to some extent, determined.

Maslow's Hierarchy of Needs

Maslow's (1943) **hierarchy of needs** is an enduring model of psychological development. First of all, the most basic human needs to be met are biological (physiological) – air, food, water, clothing, shelter, sleep, etc. Then, come safety needs which include resources, employment, family, and health; next is the need for love and belonging, from friends, family, and a sexual partner. After that comes the need for esteem including self-esteem and respect from others. Once these 'deficiency needs' have been met, people can turn their attention to **self-actualisation**, which is at the top of the hierarchy and includes, spirituality, creativity and acceptance of the world as it is.

Whilst Maslow suggested that it is often the case that individuals 'work up' through the hierarchy step-by-step, he recognised that this is not always the case for everybody. For example, someone may need to address their need for self-esteem before finding love.

Self-Actualisation

Self-actualisation is rare, but its achievement provides the possibility of true self-awareness and an honest relationship with the realities of an imperfect world. Maslow believed that self-actualisation, when it is achieved, takes the form of peak experiences which are characterised by feelings of euphoria and seeing the world with awe and wonder, without any fear or inhibitions. He cited Albert Einstein as an individual who had famously achieved self-actualisation through his creativeness.

Focus on The Self

Rogers was primarily interested in two basic human needs: the need for **self-worth** and the need for **unconditional positive regard** from other people. Both emerge from good relationships with supportive parents in childhood, and later with friends and partners. An individuals' self-worth has a direct impact on psychological well-being.

The Role of Conditions of Worth

When an individual is the recipient of unconditional positive regard, they develop **conditions of worth** as a result. Parents are often the people who provide a child with unconditional positive regard during their upbringing. However, some parents impose conditions of worth on their children meaning that they must behave in certain ways to receive this (now conditional) positive regard. Conditions of worth are a type of expectation whereby an individual feels that their approval is dependent upon meeting them in order for other people, such as parents, to see them favourably. It is possible that a person will only feel self-acceptance should they meet these conditions of worth set by others which can produce a feeling of incongruence.

Congruence

For Rogers, unhappiness and dissatisfaction were the outcomes of a psychological gap between **self-concept** (the way you think you are) and the **ideal self** (the way you would like to be). When these two concepts are incongruent, it is necessary to use defence mechanisms to provide protection against feeling negative.

On the other hand, when there is an agreement between an individual's self-concept and their ideal self, they are said to be in a state of **congruence**. However, it is uncommon for a person to be congruent all of the time, so most individuals will have, or are experiencing, some degree of incongruence.

The Influence on Counselling Psychology

It was the purpose of Rogerian therapy to close the gap of incongruence between self-concept and the ideal self, and thus allow an individual to recognise both their psychological limits and their strengths, and achieve a realistic balance between them.

Rogers believed that through taking a client-centred (person-centered) approach to counselling, an individual would be helped to make positive steps towards resolving their issues, learn a deeper understanding of themselves and, ultimately, achieve self-actualisation.

The role of the therapist in this process is to provide unconditional positive regard to the client by expressing acceptance, empathy and understanding of their condition. When the client feels sufficiently supported, their conditions of worth affecting their self-concept will dissipate enabling them to move towards their ideal self and how they want to behave, rather than how they feel that they should.

Evaluation of The Humanistic Approach

- A strength of humanistic psychology is that it has had a major influence on psychological counselling. Contemporary therapists use Rogers' ideas of unconditional positive regard and help clients work toward self-awareness. This means it is a useful theory with real-world applications. It is, in fact, impossible to imagine modern client-centred therapy without its insights and techniques.

- The evidence for the existence of Maslow's hierarchy of needs is empirically thin. This, however, is to be expected from an approach that disputes the validity of empirical research. There is some validation provided by clinical data, with some surprising confirmation from the realm of management studies (Maslow, 1965; Rogers and Roethlisberger, 1982). But the theoretical emphasis on individual achievement raises significant concerns about possible cultural bias since this is not desirable in every culture and may only be a feature of Westernised or individualistic nations.

- It is hard to scientifically test the effectiveness of humanistic counselling as it can't be done in an experimental context. People believe they benefit from counselling, and there is considerable empirical evidence available to support the effectiveness of counselling methods derived from Rogers' model, like CBT (cognitive behavioural therapy) and ACT (acceptance and commitment therapy). Since a cause-effect relationship cannot be established between the treatment and outcome - that is, the client may have recovered without the counselling - scientific certainty about the validity of the theory is almost impossible.

- Some critics argue that the humanistic approach offers an unrealistic view of human nature. They point to the more sinister aspects of human behaviour and argue that the humanistic approach focuses on 'growth-orientated' behaviour whilst ignoring an individual's capacity for self-destruction. Consequently, opponents of the approach argue that the focus on self-development overlooks possible situational forces that may provide a more realistic explanation of everyday human behaviour.

Issues and Debates

- The concept of **free will** is central to humanistic thinking. Advocates of this approach believe that behaviour is a choice, rather than determined by outside forces, and an individual can directly control and influence their own destiny.

- Likewise, the concept of **holism** is of crucial importance to the humanistic approach which attempts to answer the question of what it truly means to be fully human. Since this approach focuses in subjective human experience whilst making no attempts to generate universal laws, it favours the **idiographic** approach.

Possible Exam Questions

1. Define free will. (1 mark)

2. Define congruence in relation to the humanistic approach. (2 marks)

3. Explain what Maslow meant by 'self-actualisation'. (2 marks)

4. Describe what is meant by 'conditions of worth' according to humanistic psychologists. Support your answer with an example. (3 marks)

5. Gwion is an unhappy man in his early twenties who lacks confidence in his own abilities and physical appearance. He has been referred for counselling therapy. During his first session, his therapist suggests that Gwion lacks congruence.

   Explain what is meant by the term congruence and suggest **one** way in that Gwion might be able achieve congruence. (4 marks)
   Exam Hint: Following a coherent explanation of what is meant by the term congruence, students are likely to identify that Gwion needs to address the discrepancy between his self-concept and ideal self. This can be achieved by the therapist providing Gwion with unconditional positive regard.

6. Evaluate the influence of the humanistic approach on counselling psychology. (4 marks)

7. Explain why humanistic psychologists have avoided the scientific method. Refer to **two** key assumptions of the humanistic approach in your answer. (4 marks)
   Exam Hint: Students must avoid making generic comments and be sure to make the link to science clear in their response. Sound answers might focus on the reductionist nature of science which the humanistic approach actively avoids by taking a holistic viewpoint to explaining human behaviour.

8. Evaluate the humanistic approach in psychology. Refer to at least **one** strength and **one** limitation in your response. (6 marks)

9. Outline the psychodynamic approach. Discuss **at least one** difference between the psychodynamic approach and the humanistic approach in psychology. (8 marks)
   Exam Hint: It is important that students read the question carefully and state differences between the psychodynamic and humanistic approach, not similarities.

10. Discuss the humanistic approach in psychology. (16 marks)
    Exam Hint: In order to access the top mark bands, students need to move beyond simply naming the key concepts of the humanistic approach in psychology, such as: self, free will, hierarchy of needs and congruence by presenting effective elaboration of these features. Often, the quality of written communication in extended answers, such as this, can be weak so students must take care with their spelling, structure and clarity of expression.

11. It has been argued that the humanistic approach offers little value to psychology. Discuss the humanistic approach in psychology, referring to **at least one other** approach in your response. (16 marks)
    Exam Hint: A likely discussion points for this question is that the humanistic approach is criticised for its a lack of scientific rigour. Good answers will then be able to compare the humanistic approach with another approach on their methodology. Likewise, strengths of the approach are also creditworthy.

COMPARISON OF APPROACHES [A-LEVEL ONLY]

Specification: Comparison of approaches.

WHAT YOU NEED TO KNOW
▪ To use the issues and debates in psychology to compare and contrast the different approaches in psychology.*

The different approaches in psychology have been explored: **behaviourist, social learning theory, cognitive, biological, psychodynamic** and **humanistic**. The requirements of the specification for A-Level are to be able to compare these approaches. One way to do this is to consider the similarities and differences in terms of several key debates in psychology including their stance on **free will** versus **determinism, nature** versus **nurture, reductionism** versus **holism,** whether they adopt an **idiographic** and/or **nomothetic** approach to research.

*While this section focuses on the issues and debates as a source of comparison; additional comparisons are evident in other parts of the specification. For example, in the Attachment Topic Companion, the learning theory of attachment and Bowlby's theory of attachment are explored in relation to the nature versus nurture debate; in the Psychopathology Topic Companion: OCD is examined in relation to biological determinism; phobias in relation to environmental determinism and depression in relation to soft determinism, etc.

This chapter will demonstrate how to compare each of the Approaches in Psychology to other approaches, using various issues and debates. The purpose of this section is to demonstrate the skill of comparison and how to use the issues and debates to make effective comparisons.

Comparison of The Biological Approach with The Humanistic Approach: Reductionism Versus Holism [Difference]

The biological and humanistic approaches differ in their methodology of examining and explaining human behaviour. The biological approach attempts to break human behaviour down into different structures and processes that occur at a biological level (e.g. the function of genes, hormones, neurotransmitters, etc.) and use these biological properties to explain human behaviour. The humanistic approach argues that human behaviour should be explained at a holistic level and that the only way to understand human behaviour is to focus on all aspects of human experience. Humanistic psychologists strongly disagree with the idea of reductionism as they believe that reductionism simplifies the complex nature of human behaviour. Therefore, these two approaches radically differ in the extent to which they examine and explain human behaviour, with biological psychologists advocating a reductionist point of view and humanistic psychologists advocating a holistic point of view.

Comparison of The Behaviourist Approach with Social Learning Theory: Nature Versus Nurture [Similarity]

The behaviourist approach and social learning theory (SLT) are similar in their approach to explaining how human behaviour is shaped through reinforcement. A central tenet of operant conditioning (the behaviourist approach) is that of positive and negative reinforcement which serves to ensure that behaviour is repeated. Within SLT the notion of vicarious reinforcement is important for social learning to occur. So, whilst both approaches focus on different types of reinforcement, both recognise the importance of the environment (**nurture**) on human behaviour.

Comparison of Social Learning Theory with The Psychodynamic Approach: Free Will Versus Determinism [Difference]

SLT and the psychodynamic approach differ in the extent to which they claim that human behaviour is determined. The psychodynamic approach claims that behaviour is determined by unconscious drives and early childhood experiences, which is known as **psychic determinism**. SLT takes a softer view and claims that while behaviour is influenced by environmental forces (e.g. vicarious reinforcement), humans have personal responsibility and free choice, which is known as **soft determinism**. Therefore, these two approaches differ in their view about the extent to which humans have control over their own behaviour, with the psychodynamic approach advocating a harder view of determinism in comparison to SLT.

Comparison of The Cognitive Approach with The Psychodynamic Approach: Nomothetic Versus Idiographic Approaches [Similarity]

While the cognitive and psychodynamic approaches are different in many ways, they are similar in their methodology of examining and explaining human behaviour. The cognitive approach takes a **nomothetic approach**, generating theories (e.g. the multi-store model, the working memory model, etc.) to explain human behaviour. Furthermore, the cognitive approach makes uses of **idiographic methods** (e.g. case studies of Patient HM, KF, etc.) to provide evidence to support or refute cognitive theories. Likewise, the psychodynamic approach also takes a nomothetic approach, generating theories (e.g. psychosexual stages of development, theories of personality, etc.) to explain human behaviour, while also utilising idiographic methods (e.g. case studies of Little Hans, Rat Man, etc.) to provide evidence to support or refute psychodynamic theories. Therefore, while these approaches remain different in many ways, they both utilise nomothetic and idiographic approaches to explain and examine human behaviour.

Comparison of The Psychodynamic Approach with The Humanistic Approach: Free Will Versus Determinism [Difference]

The psychodynamic approach and humanistic approach are fundamentally different. One difference is the extent to which each approach claims that human behaviour is determined. The psychodynamic approach claims that behaviour is determined by unconscious drives and early childhood experiences, which is known as **psychic determinism**. The humanistic approach claims that humans have control over their own environment and are capable of change. Incidentally, the humanistic approach is the only approach that advocates complete **free will**. Therefore, these two approaches could not be more different in their view about the extent to which humans have control over their own behaviour.

Comparison of The Humanistic Approach with Social Learning Theory: Nature Versus Nurture [Similarity]

The humanistic approach and SLT are similar in their approach to explaining how human behaviour is shaped by the environment (nurture). From a humanistic approach, the individual strives within their environment to achieve self-actualisation. Within SLT, the notion of vicarious reinforcement is important for social learning to occur. So, whilst both approaches focus on different key contributors to shaping behaviour, both recognise the importance of nurture whereby the environment can influence the outcome of behaviour.

	FREE WILL VS. DETERMINISM	NATURE VS. NURTURE	REDUCTIONISM VS. HOLISM	IDIOGRAPHIC VS. NOMOTHETIC	SCIENTIFIC
BIOLOGICAL	**Biological Determinism** Behaviour is controlled by internal biological factors (e.g. genes, hormones, neurotransmitters, etc).	**Nature** Behaviour is the result of innate biological factors (e.g. genes, hormones, neurotransmitters, etc).	**Biological Reductionism** Behaviour is broken down into biological structures/processes.	**Nomothetic** Creates universal laws, as humans share similar physiologies.	**Scientific** The biological approach promotes scientific methods of investigation (e.g. brain imaging)
BEHAVIOURIST	**Environmental Determinism** Behaviour is controlled by stimulus-response conditioning.	**Nurture** Humans are born as a tabula rasa (blank slate) and behaviour is learned.	**Environmental Reductionism** Behaviour is broken down into simple stimulus-response associations.	**Nomothetic** Creates universal laws, as behaviour is the result of stimulus-response associations.	**Scientific** The behaviourist approach utilises scientific methods of investigation (e.g. laboratory experiments and animal research).
SOCIAL LEARNING	**Determinism (Soft)** Behaviour is controlled by environmental forces. However, humans have personal responsibility and free choice.	**Nurture** Behaviour is learnt from observation and vicarious reinforcement.	**Partially Reductionist** This approach shares elements of the behaviourist and cognitive approaches.	**Nomothetic** Attempts to establish general laws of behaviour (e.g. vicarious reinforcement).	**Mostly Scientific** Utilises scientific methods but also takes into account mediational processes.
COGNITIVE	**Determinism (Soft)** Behaviour is controlled by mediational processes; however, humans can choose what information they attend to.	**Nature & Nurture** Behaviour is the product of information processing and modified by experience.	**Experimental Reductionism** Behaviour is investigated in terms of isolated variables (e.g. capacity of STM).	**Nomothetic & Idiographic** Attempts to establish general laws of cognitive processing but utilises an idiographic approach with case studies.	**Mostly Scientific** Utilises scientific methods of investigation; however, researchers are unable to directly observe cognitive processes.
PSYCHODYNAMIC	**Psychic Determinism** Behaviour is determined by unconscious drives and early childhood experiences.	**Mostly Nature** Behaviour is the product of innate drives, but shaped by early childhood experiences.	**Reductionism & Holism** Behaviour is reduced to innate drives, while taking into account the multiple aspects of human behaviour.	**Nomothetic & Idiographic** Attempts to establish general laws in relation to innate drives, while considering unique experience (during childhood).	**Not Scientific** Examines many concepts/theories which cannot be empirically tested. Relies on subjective interpretation.
HUMANISTIC	**Free Will** Humans control their own environment and are capable of change.	**Mostly Nurture** Behaviour is shaped by the environment as humans strive to achieve self-actualisation.	**Holism** Focuses on understanding all aspects of human experience and interaction.	**Idiographic** Focuses on the subjective human experience and makes no attempt to create general laws.	**Not Scientific** Rejects scientific methods and is therefore unable to provide empirical evidence.

Exam Hint: When students are presented with an exam questions which demands a comparison of approaches they must ensure that any evaluation presented is not generic to one of the approaches, as this is not creditworthy, and instead explain comparative points between the two (or more) approaches. These types of essays often highlight the need for students to allow planning time before beginning their essay to ensure that their answer addresses the question set in a clear and coherent manner.

Possible Exam Questions

1. Briefly **outline** one similarity between social learning theory and any other approach in psychology. (2 marks)

Exam Hint: Since this is only a two-mark question the first mark is earned by simply identifying a similarity between social learning theory and any other approach in psychology. The second mark is gained for elaborating on this such as Social learning theory is similar to the behaviourist approach in psychology since both recognise the importance of reinforcement in shaping behaviour - positive and negative reinforcement is important in operant conditioning (behaviourist approach) and vicarious reinforcement is central to social learning. Another creditworthy similarity could be explained with reference to the cognitive approach and the role of mental processes in human learning.

2. Explain one way in which the behaviourist approach and the social learning approach in psychology are similar. (3 marks)

3. Briefly explain two similarities that exist between the humanistic approach in psychology and the psychodynamic approach to explaining human behaviour. (4 marks)

4. Briefly outline **two** differences between the behaviourist approach in psychology and the cognitive approach. (4 marks)

5. Outline **two** differences between the humanistic approach in psychology and the cognitive approach. (6 marks)

6. Critics of the humanistic approach claim it has little to offer psychology. Discuss the humanistic approach, referring to at least **one** other approach in your response. (16 marks)

Exam Hint: Likely comparison points to draw between the humanistic approach and others in psychology could relate to concepts such as free will (versus determinism) and scientific methodology (or lack thereof). Valid comparisons will often refer to the behaviourist and/or psychodynamic approach.

7. Discuss what makes the psychodynamic approach unique in psychology with reference to other approaches in your response. (16 marks)

Exam Hint: Questions such as this really highlight the limitations of learning essay answers by rote. In order to access the higher mark bands here, any answer must be tailored to meet the specific demands of the question in regard to what makes the psychodynamic approach unique, rather than a simple outline and evaluate/discuss response.

8. Describe the humanistic approach in psychology and discuss differences between this approach and the psychodynamic approach. (16 marks)

9. Outline the biological approach in psychology. Compare the biological approach to the behaviourist approach to explaining human behaviour. (16 marks)

10. Discuss social learning theory. In your response, draw comparisons with at least **one** other approach in psychology. (16 marks)

Exam Hint: A pitfall for many students on this question is the tendency to evaluate research into social learning theory, such as the Bobo doll experiment. This, however, is not creditworthy in this context since the question is asking for the evaluation commentary to be made upon comparisons with another approach of the students choice.

11. Describe the humanistic approach in psychology. Compare the humanistic approach with **either** the biological approach or the cognitive approach. (16 marks)

12. Describe and compare **two** approaches of your choice in psychology. (16 marks)

Discuss the contribution of behaviourist psychologists such as Pavlov and Skinner to our understanding of human behaviour. (16 marks)

Behaviourism is one of the most influential approaches in modern psychology. Its central claim is that almost all human behaviour is the result of learning. To explore the learning process, behaviourists favoured the laboratory experiment over other methods because this kind of research was objective. i.e. it focused on observable events, and could be rigorously controlled.

One of the first behaviourists to explore the relationship between learning and behaviour was Ivan Pavlov. Pavlov developed the theory of classical conditioning and famously tested it using his dogs, who were conditioned to associate the sound of a bell with food. This resulted in the dogs producing a salivation response at the sound of a bell even when no food was present. Pavlov demonstrated that repeated exposure to an event leads to a learned and uncontrollable behaviour.

Developing these ideas, B.F. Skinner suggested that behaviour was the result of learning through the consequences of our actions. Skinner conducted research into his operant conditioning theory using rats, and found that three types of consequences will affect behaviour: Positive reinforcement involves rewarding a behaviour, which increases the likelihood of it being repeated; negative reinforcement involves removing an unpleasant outcome to increase the likelihood of a behaviour being repeated; punishment involves adding an unpleasant outcome to a behaviour, which reduces the likelihood of it being repeated. For Skinner, behaviour is the result of learning and remembering the consequences of previous behaviours.

Behaviourists have significantly contributed to the still-developing recognition of psychology as a science. The experimental methods used by Pavlov and Skinner rejected the earlier emphasis in psychology on introspection and encouraged research that focused on more objective, because more measurable, dimensions of behaviour. According to behaviourists, this emphasis on the scientific method has led to an increasingly valid and reliable understanding of human behaviour. These methods have also helped psychology gain credibility and status as a scientific discipline, which in turn attracts more funding and research opportunities.

The behaviourist approach was also influential in encouraging the use of animals as research subjects. Behaviourists believed that the learning processes in humans and animals are very similar; consequently, Pavlov conducted research using dogs, and Skinner used rats and pigeons. Using non-human animals in research gives experimenters more control over the process, without demand characteristics or individual differences influencing findings. However, many consider using animals in experiments to be unethical as there is less concern about protection from harm for non-human subjects. Furthermore, some argue that findings from animal experiments are not generalizable to human behaviour: Skinner's operant conditioning theory may provide an understanding of rat behaviour, but little about human behaviour. From this perspective, behaviourists have arguably made a limited contribution to explaining human behaviour, as the biology, experiences, and capabilities of different species are extremely different.

Finally, the behavioural approach has made important contributions to our modern understanding of mental illness. For example, many phobias are thought to be the result of earlier unpleasant learning experiences. Consequently, this understanding has helped psychologists develop therapies, such as systematic desensitisation, that attempt to re-condition a patient's fear response. Also, some addictions such as gambling can be better understood through operant conditioning, as the rewards of gambling could be seen to reinforce the destructive behaviour. This demonstrates that the behaviourist approach has many real-world applications in the understanding and treatment of atypical behaviour.

[~550 Words]
Examiner style comments: *Mark band 4*

This is a well-detailed an accurate account of the behaviourist approach and its contribution to psychology. The evaluation is well-detailed, thorough and effective drawing on a range of points. The use of specialist terminology is excellent and add clarity and focus to the essay.

Outline and evaluate the social learning approach in psychology. (16 marks)

Social learning theory (SLT) rests on the idea of observational learning: that learning occurs through the observation and imitation of behaviour performed by models in the social environment. Unlike the behaviourist approach from which it derives, SLT recognises the importance of cognitive processing of informational stimuli (mediational processes) and rejects the notion that learning is purely the outcome of a stimulus-response loop.

As its name implies, learning is a social phenomenon. In order for it to take place, someone must model an attitude or behaviour in a context defined by four distinct characteristics: attention, retention, reproduction, and motivation. If these factors are implemented, imitation (i.e. copying of what has been observed) can take place; if the observed behaviour is rewarded, imitation is more likely. This learning from the observation of others' rewards is what Bandura called vicarious learning. There is also evidence (Shutts et al., 2010) to suggest that for children, the age and gender similarity to models is an important determinant of the likelihood of imitation. This cognitive appraisal process clearly distinguishes SLT from the more deterministic behaviourist approach.

One strength of SLT is its plentiful research support. For example, Fox and Bailenson (2009) found that humans were more likely to imitate computer-generated 'virtual humans' who were similar to themselves; Rushton and Campbell (1977) found that same-sex modelling significantly increased the number of female observers who agreed to, and then actually did, donate blood; and Myers (2015) confirmed the importance of vicarious learning for the effectiveness of workplace teams. These studies demonstrate support for different aspects of SLT, including modelling and vicarious reinforcement, adding credibility to the key principles of this theory.

Another strength of SLT is its applicability to real-world issues. It has long been a feature in explanations of criminal behaviour (Sykes and Matza, 1957) and recent research has continued that focus (Akers, 1998). It has also been used to examine and evaluate the effectiveness of advertising: Andsager et al. (2006) found that 'identification with a character or example may increase the likelihood that audiences will model behaviour presented in an anti-alcohol message'. Consequently, the principles of SLT can be used to provide a positive impact on promotional health campaigns, and indirectly help combat problem behaviours like alcoholism.

However, one limitation of SLT revolves around the issue of causality: Do people learn behaviour from models, or do they seek out models who exhibit behaviour or attitudes they already favour? Siegel and McCormick (2006), for example, argue that young people who hold deviant values and attitudes are more likely to associate with similarly-inclined peers because they are more fun to be with, and thus the reinforcement of 'deviant' behaviour is a two-way process and not necessarily the result of SLT itself. Also, SLT struggles to explain complex behaviours like gender development. Children are exposed to a whole host of influences when growing up, and these different influences interact in a complex way. Consequently, it is difficult to distinguish behaviours that develop because of SLT from the many other factors that contribute to human behaviour, which poses an issue for the social learning explanation of behaviour.

[~525 Words]
Examiner style comments: *Mark band 4*

This is a well-structured and clear essay which provides an accurate and well-detailed account of SLT and a range of effective evaluation to critique this theory. The essay is clear, coherent and focused and specialist terminology is used throughout.

Sammi and Krishna are talking. Sammi says, 'Look at your little sister Josephine. She's pretending she's got an iPhone and is sending a text message.'

Krishna replies, 'Yes. But when Josephine saw me get told off for using my Dad's iPad, she never copied me doing that!'

Describe and evaluate social learning theory. Refer to the conversation above as part of your answer. (16 marks)

Social learning theory (SLT) rests on the idea of observational learning: that learning occurs through the observation and imitation of behaviour performed by role models in a social environment. As its name implies, learning is a social phenomenon. In order for learning to take place, someone must model an attitude or behaviour in a context defined by four mediational processes: attention, retention, reproduction, and motivation.

In this scenario, Krishna is acting as a role model to her little sister, Josephine, who has clearly paid attention to her older sister. Josephine has retained this behaviour and reproduced it by pretending that she has an iPhone of her own. Finally, Josephine is motivated to carry out this action because her older sister is seen as a role model and it is likely that she looks up to her.

In addition, Josephine has also learned via vicarious reinforcement. She has seen her older sister, Krishna, get told off for using her Dad's iPad (vicarious punishment) and does not copy this behaviour because she does not want to be punished in the same way.

One strength of SLT comes from research support. For example, Rushton and Campbell (1977) found that same-sex modelling significantly increased the number of female observers who agreed to, and then actually did, donate blood. This study demonstrates support for the idea of same-sex modelling, adding credibility to this component of SLT. Furthermore, this study also explains why Josephine imitates her older sister, as Krishna is a same-sex role model which increases the likelihood of imitation taking place.

Another strength of SLT is its applicability to real-world issues. For example, SLT has also been used to examine and evaluate the effectiveness of advertising: Andsager et al. (2006) found that 'identification with a character or example may increase the likelihood that audiences will model behaviour presented in an anti-alcohol message'. Consequently, the principles of SLT can be used to provide a positive impact on promotional health campaigns, and indirectly help combat problem behaviours like alcoholism.

However, one limitation of SLT revolves around the issue of causality: Do people learn behaviour from models, or do they seek out models who exhibit behaviour or attitudes they already favour? In this case, it is not clear whether Josephine has learned from her sister Krishna, or whether she seeks out Krishna because they are similar in terms of having a family connection. Siegel and McCormick (2006), for example, argue that young people who hold deviant values and attitudes are more likely to associate with similarly-inclined peers because they are more fun to be with, and thus the reinforcement of 'deviant' behaviour is a two-way process and not necessarily the result of SLT itself. Consequently, it is difficult to distinguish behaviours that develop because of SLT from the many other factors that contribute to human behaviour, which poses an issue for the social learning explanation of behaviour.

[~525 Words]
Examiner style comments: *Mark band 4*

This is a well-structured and clear essay which provides an accurate and well-detailed account of SLT while applying the knowledge and the evaluation (in most cases) to Josephine. The essay is clear, coherent and focused and specialist terminology is used throughout. The application is appropriate, and the links to the STEM are explained well.

Outline and evaluate the cognitive approach in psychology. (16 marks)

The cognitive approach focuses on the examination of mental processes: perception, memory, attention, consciousness. Because these processes are internal, they cannot be studied directly; instead, their operation must be inferred from the observation and measurement of visible human behaviour.

To assist this inference, cognitive psychologists make use of theoretical models. Models enable the representation of complex conceptual processes so that their components can be better understood. An example of this is the multi-store model of memory which presents a picture of memory based on an information-processing analogy. Theoretical models also provide a basis for research.

Schema theory is another information-processing model that emphasises how perception and memory are shaped by cognitive frameworks built from experience that organise and interpret information in the brain. Schemas allow us to make sense of an often ambiguous world by "filling in the gaps" in our knowledge and thus enable us to act comfortably even when our information is incomplete.

Recent advances in neuroimaging technology, such as Function Magnetic Resonance Imaging (fMRI), have lent weight to theoretical models by providing empirical confirmation of brain activity for specific cognitive functions under controlled conditions. However, the precise meaning of this activity is still a matter for debate. Some claim that these techniques provide the cognitive approach with a strong scientific grounding, while others insist that neuroimaging evidence is only correlational, and therefore does not constitute true scientific validation of either theories or models. Nevertheless, the availability of such techniques and their increasing sophistication is one clear strength of the cognitive approach.

Another strength of the cognitive approach is its recognition of the complexity of human behaviour, and thus its hesitation to assert a reductionist explanation of mental processes. There can be no doubt that all cognition rests on a biological foundation since it occurs in the brain and is made possible by its operation. But the precise nature of consciousness and memory and perception are not easily reducible to purely biological outcomes, as the lived experience of all human beings seems to consistently demonstrate.

Ironically, this appreciation of cognitive complexity can also be a weakness of the approach. Not all human behaviour can be captured under the cognitive umbrella; the research in this field has tended to neglect other significant dimensions of behaviour such as emotion and motivation which may be linked to cognition, but are not the same. The cognitive approach is careful to insist that we are more than biological machines, but often overlooks the equally important fact that we are not only cognitive creatures.

A third strength of the cognitive approach derives from this 'soft determinist' ontology: It has many real-world applications. For example, cognitive research into memory and the effects of misleading information has reduced the use of eyewitness testimony in court cases, and led to major reforms in police procedure, like the use of the cognitive interview. Additionally, a better understanding of thinking patterns has helped professionals understand and treat mental illnesses such as depression through the use of therapies like CBT. This indicates that cognitive research has made concrete contributions to contemporary society and has developed professional understanding in many fields.

[~525 words]
Examiner style comments: *Mark band 4*

This is a well-detailed essay which explains the many components of the cognitive approach accurately. The evaluation is generally effective; however, the final evaluation point exceptionally concludes the essay and reinforces the effective nature of the evaluation overall. The use of specialist terminology is consistent throughout.

Outline and evaluate the biological approach in psychology. (16 marks)

The biological approach assumes that all human behaviour has a biological origin. This approach insists that to fully comprehend human behaviour, it is necessary to understand internal biological structures and processes such as genes, the nervous system, and neurochemistry.

Geneticists working within this approach have found evidence that some behavioural characteristics, such as intelligence or mental illness, can be inherited in a similar way to physical characteristics, such as eye colour. A large amount of research in this area has used Monozygotic (MZ) twins because they share 100% of their DNA. For example, recent research has found that MZ twins have an increased concordance rate of developing schizophrenia compared to Dizygotic twins. This is important to understanding the genetic component of mental illness and demonstrates the impact of genes on certain behaviours.

The influence of neurochemistry is also explored in the biological approach. Research in this realm helps us understand the role of neurotransmitters. For example, recent research suggests that abnormally low levels of serotonin are linked to aggressive behaviour, indicating that this neurotransmitter is important in regulating behaviour and impulse control (Crockett et al., 2008).

One weakness of the biological approach is that causation is often strongly implied in explanations that focus on brain structures. For example, one explanation of schizophrenia suggests that a lack of activity in the ventral striatum is linked to the development of negative symptoms such as avolition. This is a problem for biological explanations because such research tells us only that there is an association between brain structures and behaviour; it cannot tell us that the reduced activity in that area of the brain causes the behaviour, or that the behaviour causes lower activity in that part of the brain. Therefore, it is critically important to remember that biological explanations are often based on correlational results, which does not mean that one event causes the other.

However, the biological approach is also known for using more reliable methods of research. For example, some research into genetics and neurochemistry requires precise scientific methodology, such as fMRIs, PET scans, drug trials, and EEGs. These techniques provide psychologists with an accurate measure of internal processes that previously were not accessible. This makes biological evidence less susceptible to misinterpretation or experimenter bias which is a strength of such research.

The second weakness of this approach is that many biological explanations of human behaviour may be considered deterministic. For example, another assumption of the biological approach is that some human behaviours are the result of evolution: they maximise our chances of survival and reproduction, and thus are 'naturally selected' and inherited from our ancestors. Such evolutionary claims are used to explain a variety of gender differences in human behaviour including sexual selection, aggression, and stress. Such explanations imply that humans have little control over their behaviour, and suggest we are predetermined to act in a certain way regardless of experience, free will, or the environment. This is problematic for those who do not follow 'typical' or 'expected' behaviours and overemphasises the role of nature on behaviour. It is also an explanation that is unfalsifiable, and thus incapable of scientific validation.

A final advantage of the biological approach is that it has many real-world applications: Drug therapies have been developed for many mental illnesses based on research into neurotransmitters; antidepressants work to increase serotonin levels in the brain, based on the understanding of how low levels of serotonin contribute to depressive symptoms. Understanding 'abnormal' neurochemical activity in the brain has not only been helpful for developing treatments but has also provided patients with an explanation that their illness is not their fault.

[~600 words]
Examiner style comments: *Mark band 4*

This is a highly detailed and accurate essay examining the biological approach. The use of specialist terminology, including key issues and debates, is impressive, and the evaluation was focused, thorough and effective. Overall, an impressive account of the biological approach.

Outline and evaluate the psychodynamic approach in psychology. (16 marks)

The foundation of psychodynamic thinking in psychology was laid by Sigmund Freud. Freud discovered (or invented) the notion of the unconscious which lies at the root of his hugely influential psychoanalytic method. Freud's theories revolve around three central ideas: that personality has a discernible structure; that it is constructed by the passage through psychosexual stages; and that the unconscious conflicts of this process are mediated by psychological processes he called defence mechanisms.

According to Freud, personality has three components. The id is pure erotic energy: It is governed by primal urges that Freud called drives, and seeks nothing but pleasure. The ego is governed by the reality principle and is tasked with taming the id. The ego is conscious and aware of the demands of others outside of the self. It does not exist in the infant who is a creature of the id alone. But it arises in response to the control over desires exercised by others, especially parents. The superego is conscience, that inner voice that tells us when we have transgressed the bounds of acceptable behaviour: It is the internalised parent and comes into being reluctantly in response parental discipline.

The road to conscience passes through the psychosexual stages: oral, anal, phallic, and genital. In each stage, the child has its desires for bodily pleasure denied and redirected by its parents until they focus exclusively on the appropriate sexual outlet. The driver of this complex process is the Oedipus complex in which boys relinquish their desire for their mother, and internalise the fear of castration by their father as the cautionary voice of conscience. This process is traumatic, and cannot be confronted directly, and so the ego establishes defence mechanisms, like repression and denial, to mediate the psychological terrors it generates.

As strange as Freud's ideas may seem now, they have been enormously influential in both the practice of psychology and in our understanding of how culture operates. The evidence for these ideas is almost entirely clinical rather than empirical, and its scientific credibility is questionable. But few would deny that there are, in fact, unconscious motivations and demonstrable defence mechanisms, and these existential realities have allowed Freudian theory to maintain some hold on psychotherapeutic techniques, like psychoanalysis, which is still used to treat patients today. Furthermore, there is empirical research to support the efficacy of psychoanalysis. Biskup et al. (2005) reported a naturalistic study of 36 patients that demonstrated that at the end of psychoanalytic therapy, 77% of the patients showed clinically significant improvements. Bachrach et al. (2000) conducted a meta-analysis of every major study of the efficacy of psychoanalytic treatment and found that all the studies show that psychoanalysis is an effective treatment for many patients.

Freud's theories are very much products of their time and place. Their obsession with the Oedipus complex is intensely androcentric, and many would claim this makes them irrelevant to an understanding of women. But female psychoanalysts like Melanie Klein and Nancy Chodorow have shown that even gender-biased theories can be adopted to provide useful insights into human behaviour. However, the culture-bias of psychoanalytic theory is perhaps more profound. All of Freud's patients came from the Viennese middle-class, and his universal generalisations were based on this highly unrepresentative sample. He called his therapy "the talking cure", and there is considerable evidence to suggest that it is only suitable for cultures where the discussion of personal problems is encouraged. This is more a practical limitation than a conceptual one, but it casts some doubt on the effectiveness of any therapeutic approach based on psychoanalytic ideas.

[~600 Words]
Examiner style comments: *Mark band 4*

This essay demonstrates an exceptionally clear understanding and appreciation of psychodynamic psychology. The knowledge is excellent, and the evaluation is thorough, effective, interesting and focused on the demands of the question. The evaluation draws on suitable issues and debates, and research evidence to provide an interesting commentary.

Outline and evaluate the humanistic approach in psychology. (16 marks)

Humanistic psychology is intensively focused on one ontological question: What does it mean to be fully human? It recognises the importance and insights of cognitive neuroscience and systematic empirical research but insists that all other approaches are partial and reductionist, and that only its fluid boundaries of theory and practice can provide the conceptual space in which the holistic complexity of human behaviour can be understood.

There are many strands of humanistic psychology, but all draw on the work of the field's founding figures, Abraham Maslow and Carl Rogers. Maslow's (1943) famous hierarchy of needs is an enduring model of psychological development: The most basic needs are biological – air, food, water, clothing, shelter, sleep; then come safety needs, which include resources, employment, family, and health; next is the need for love and belonging, from friends, family, and a sexual partner. After that comes the need for esteem, both self-esteem and respect from others. Once these 'deficiency needs' have been met, people can turn their attention to self-actualisation, which includes, spirituality, creativity and acceptance of the world as it is. Self-actualisation is rare, but its achievement provides the possibility of true self-awareness and an honest relationship with the realities of an always-imperfect world.

The evidence for the existence of this hierarchy is empirically thin, as would be expected from an approach that disputes the validity of empirical research. There is some validation provided by clinical data, and some surprising confirmation from the realm of management studies (Maslow, 1965; Rogers and Roethlisberger, 1982). But the theoretical emphasis on individual achievement raises significant concerns about possible cultural bias.

Rogers was primarily interested in just two basic needs: the need for self-worth and the need for unconditional positive regard from other people. Both emerge from good relationships with supportive parents in childhood, and later with friends and partners. For Rogers, unhappiness and dissatisfaction were the outcomes of a psychological gap between self-concept (the way you think you are) and ideal self (the way you would like to be. When these were congruent, people were healthy; when they weren't, and this was true for most people most of the time, it was necessary to use defence mechanisms to provide protection against feeling bad. It was the purpose of Rogerian therapy to close this gap, and thus allow the troubled individual to recognise both their psychological limits and their strengths, and achieve a realistic balance between them.

Humanistic psychology has had a major influence on psychological counselling, and contemporary therapists use Rogers' ideas of unconditional positive regard to help clients work toward self-awareness. This means it is a useful theory with real-world applications: It is, in fact, impossible to imagine modern client-centred therapy without its insights and techniques.

However, it is hard to scientifically test the effectiveness of humanistic counselling as it can't be done in an experimental context. People believe they benefit from counselling, and there is considerable empirical evidence available to support the effectiveness of counselling methods derived from Rogers' model, like CBT and ACT. But since one cannot establish a cause-effect relationship between treatment and outcome (i.e. the client may have recovered without the counselling), a narrowly scientific certainty about the validity of the theory is probably impossible. Furthermore, some critics argue that the humanistic approach offers an unrealistic view of human nature. Critics point to the more sinister aspects of human behaviour and argue that humanism focuses on 'growth-orientated' behaviour while ignoring individual capacity for self-destruction. Consequently, such critics argue that a focus on self-development ignores situational forces that may provide a more realistic explanation of everyday human behaviour.

[~600 Words]
Examiner style comments: *Mark band 4*

This is a well-detailed and accurate account of humanistic psychology, referring to the two key theorists, Maslow and Rogers. The evaluation is thorough and effective in most places, and the final paragraph provides an interesting high-level discussion of the humanistic approach.

Harriette's mother and father are worried about her mobile found use. Harriette is becoming increasingly anxious and has low self-esteem. However, Harriette does feel good when she receives WhatsApp messages or 'likes' on Facebook; holding and using her iPhone make her feel safe. Harriette's mother and father are worried that her reliance on her iPhone and how this is affecting her work at school, as well as her well-being.

Outline and evaluate the humanistic approach. Refer to Harriette's behaviour in your answer. (16 marks)

There are many strands of humanistic psychology, but all draw on the work of Maslow and Rogers. Maslow's (1943) famous hierarchy of needs is an enduring model of psychological development: the most basic needs are biological – food, water, clothing, shelter, sleep; then come safety needs, which include resources, employment, family, and health; next is the need for love and belonging, from friends, family, etc. After that comes the need for esteem, both self-esteem and respect from others. Harriette has low self-esteem; she is unable to progress any further up the hierarchy of needs until she fulfils these needs and therefore she is unable to self-actualise. According to Maslow, once these 'deficiency needs' have been met, people can turn their attention to self-actualisation, which includes, spirituality, creativity and acceptance of the world as it is.

The evidence for the existence of the hierarchy of needs is empirically thin, as would be expected from an approach that disputes the validity of empirical research. Some of the concepts within the hierarchy of needs (e.g. self-actualisation) are difficult to operationalise and therefore very difficult to test empirically. Furthermore, as humanistic psychologists are typically against nomothetic methods of investigation, providing any research support for these abstract concepts becomes difficult if not impossible. Consequently, psychologists are unable to provide any research support for the existence of the hierarchy of needs and other aspects of humanistic psychology making such theories/concepts questionable.

Rogers was primarily interested in just two basic needs: the need for self-worth and the need for unconditional positive regard from other people. Both emerge from good relationships with supportive parents in childhood, and later with friends and partners. For Rogers, unhappiness and dissatisfaction were the outcomes of a psychological gap between self-concept (the way you think you are) and ideal self (the way you would like to be). Harriette may be experiencing a gap between her self-concept (e.g. she is anxious) and her ideal self (e.g. feeling good from receiving WhatsApp messages and Facebook 'likes'). According to Rogers, when these concepts are congruent, people are healthy; when they are not, as in Harriette's case, it is necessary to use defence mechanisms to provide protection against feeling bad.

One strength of Humanistic psychology is that it has had a major influence on psychological counselling. For example, many contemporary therapists use Rogers' ideas of unconditional positive regard to help clients work toward self-awareness. This means it is a useful theory with real-world applications and has helped improve the outlook of many patients, providing them support with their psychological issues.

Furthermore, many psychologists praise the humanistic approach for its positive and holistic focus. Humanistic psychologists, unlike other psychologists, do not try to reduce behaviour and experience to simpler component parts. For example, biological psychologists reduce psychological disorders to neurochemical imbalances and/or genetic inheritance. In stark contrast, humanistic psychologists argue for a holistic view of human nature. It is the only approach that attempts to consider all aspects of human nature in a holistic manner while promoting free will and human choice.

However, some critics argue that the humanistic approach offers an unrealistic view of human nature. Critics point to the more sinister aspects of human behaviour and argue that humanism focuses on 'growth-orientated' behaviour while ignoring individual capacity for self-destruction. Consequently, such critics argue that a focus on self-development ignores situational forces that may provide a more realistic explanation of everyday human behaviour.

[~550 Words]
Examiner style comments: *Mark band 4*

A well-detailed and accurate essay that outlines numerous strands of humanistic psychology. The evaluation is plentiful and thorough and effective, and the application to Harriette is appropriate. Further application would have been possible; however, this answer has remained effective by presenting a wealth of knowledge and evaluation.

Outline the key features of the cognitive approach in psychology. Compare the cognitive approach with the psychodynamic approach. (16 marks)

The cognitive approach focuses on the examination of mental processes: perception, memory, attention, consciousness. Because these processes are internal, they cannot be studied directly; instead, their operation must be inferred from the observation and measurement of visible human behaviour.

To assist this inference, cognitive psychologists make use of theoretical models. Models enable the representation of complex conceptual processes so that their components can be better understood. An example of this is the multi-store model of memory which presents a picture of memory based on an information-processing analogy. Theoretical models also provide a basis for research.

Schema theory is another information-processing model that emphasises how perception and memory are shaped by cognitive frameworks built from experience that organise and interpret information in the brain. Schemas allow us to make sense of an often ambiguous world by "filling in the gaps" in our knowledge, and thus enable us to act comfortably even when our information is incomplete.

Though profoundly different in fundamental ways, the cognitive and psychodynamic approaches do share some unexpected similarities. Both seek nomothetic conclusions about human behaviour, i.e. general laws that can be applied universally. For example, the cognitive models of memory are not specific to populations or locations, and Freud believed his psychosexual stages of development were applicable to all people always. But important evidence for these nomothetic claims is derived in both approaches from case studies: For cognitive psychology, the cases of HM and Clive Wearing are indispensable support for the multi-store model of memory; for psychodynamic psychology, the case study is the primary source of data, as illustrated by Freud's classic monographs on the Wolf Man and Little Hans. These case studies provide rich data to confirm the presence of internal processes unavailable to direct observation, but suffer from the lack of generalizability common to such idiographic accounts, and thus are susceptible to the charge that they do not meet the standards of scientific credibility.

Another similarity between the cognitive and psychodynamic approach is that both recognize the influence of experience on our behaviour in later life. According to the cognitive understanding of schemas, past experiences provide the content of the mental representations that inform our expectations of future events, and thus shape our perception of them and our responses to them. This can, of course, lead to the development of stereotypes, and the subsequent disregard for information that does not fit our pre-existing frameworks of knowledge. The psychodynamic approach likewise places great emphasis on the role of childhood experiences in the shaping of adult behaviour. For example, Freud suggested that unresolved conflict that develops during our passage through the psychosexual stages could cause fixations in later life, and the psychological unease that is their result. This demonstrates that both approaches acknowledge the importance of nurture on the operation of internal mental processes. This could indicate, however, that both approaches are limited by a form of determinism, soft determinism for the cognitive approach, and a much stronger psychic determinism for the psychodynamic approach.

A final similarity is that both have been practically applied to help people in the real world. The cognitive understanding has enabled psychologists to clinically address psychopathology, i.e. why faulty thinking may lead to psychological disorders; from this has developed treatments, such as CBT, to help people recognise and challenge distorted thinking patterns. Psychodynamic therapy in the form of psychoanalysis has been a central feature in the history of psychiatry as a medical speciality. This therapy can include hypnosis, dream analysis, and other techniques aimed at accessing the unconscious. Whilst this therapy has reduced in popularity over the past few decades, the psychodynamic approach has been an influential element in the development of later therapies such as CBT.

[~625 Words]
Examiner style comments: *Mark band 4*

This is an excellent response to this complex question. The answer provides detailed knowledge of the cognitive approach which is highly accurate. Furthermore, the discussion is centred on three similarities and provides an in-depth commentary that is thorough and effective, with an excellent use of specialist terminology.

Outline the biological approach in psychology. Compare the biological approach to the behaviourist approach to explaining human behaviour. (16 marks)

The biological approach assumes that all human behaviour has a biological origin. This approach insists that to fully comprehend human behaviour, it is necessary to understand internal biological structures and processes such as genes, the nervous system, and neurochemistry.

Geneticists working within this approach have found evidence that some behavioural characteristics, such as intelligence or mental illness, can be inherited in a similar way to physical characteristics, such as eye colour. A large amount of research in this area has used Monozygotic (MZ) twins because they share 100% of their DNA. For example, recent research has found that MZ twins have an increased concordance rate of developing schizophrenia compared to Dizygotic twins. This is important to understanding the genetic component of mental illness and demonstrates the impact of genes on certain behaviours.

The influence of neurochemistry is also explored in the biological approach. Research in this realm helps us understand the role of neurotransmitters. For example, recent research suggests that abnormally low levels of serotonin are linked to aggressive behaviour, indicating that this neurotransmitter is important in regulating behaviour and impulse control (Crockett et al., 2008).

One similarity between the biological and behaviourist approaches is the view that behaviour is determined. The biological approach suggests that behaviour is controlled by internal biological factors (e.g. genes and hormones) and as a result, humans have little choice in their behaviour. The behaviourist approach suggests that behaviour is controlled by stimulus-response conditioning (e.g. through classical and/or operant conditioning). As a result, both approaches suggest that humans have little free will and choice in their behaviour, with the biological approach advocating biological determinism and the behaviourist approach advocating environmental determinism.

Another similarity between the biological and behaviourist approaches is their approach to investigating human behaviour. Both approaches take a nomothetic approach and attempt to create universal laws of behaviour that apply to all humans. Furthermore, both approaches favour a reductionist point of view, with biological psychologists breaking behaviour down in simple biological structures and processes (known as biological reductionism) and behaviourist psychologists breaking behaviour in simple stimulus-response associations (environmental reductionism). Therefore, while their theories are fundamentally different, their approach to examining and explaining human behaviour is both reductionist and nomothetic.

However, one difference between the biological and behaviourist approaches is their position in relation to the nature-nurture debate. Biological psychologists suggest that behaviour is the result of innate biological factors (e.g. genes and neurotransmitters) and therefore suggest a nature-based view of behaviour. Behaviourist psychologists, on the other hand, suggest that humans are born a blank slate (tabula rasa) and behaviour is learned, which is a nurture-based view of behaviour. Therefore, despite their similarities in terms of determinism, nomothetic approaches and reductionism, these two approaches sit are opposite ends of the nature-nurture debate.

[~450 Words]
Examiner style comments: *Mark band 4*

This is a well-detailed and accurate essay which provides a solid outline of the biological approach. The essay provides a thorough and effective comparison of the biological and behaviourist approaches, centred on the issues and debates in psychology. An impressive use of a range of specialist terminology is presented throughout.

Approaches in Psychology	The Approaches in Psychology topic considers the different beliefs of psychologists who make up the different approaches. These include behavioural psychologists, cognitive psychologists, social learning theorists, biological psychologists, psychodynamic psychologists and humanistic psychologists. Each of these different approaches has its own view of human behaviour and how to conduct psychological research.
Bandura	Albert Bandura developed Social Learning Theory and conducted experiments into observational learning using the Bobo doll. While agreeing that humans could learn through classical and operant conditioning, he also argued that they could learn through observation and imitation.
Behaviourist Approach	The behaviourist approach attempts to explain behaviour in terms of learning. Behaviourists study changes in behaviour that are caused by a person's direct experience of their environment, using the principles of classical and operant conditioning. They are determined to be **scientific** and therefore refuse to discuss mental processes that might be involved in learning, because they are not observable and cannot be studied objectively.
Biological Approach	The biological approach attempts to explain behaviour in terms of different biological processes, including genes, hormones, neurotransmitters, etc. According to the biological approach, the brain and the mind are identical, and brain physiology and biochemical imbalances can affect behaviour. Biological psychologists also believe that behaviour can be inherited, as it is determined by genetic information.
Biological Structures	In relation to the biological approach in psychology, biological structures are organs (such as the brain) and systems (such as the nervous system) that influence human behaviour.
Classical Conditioning: Approaches in Psychology	**Classical conditioning** is a type of learning discovered by Ivan Pavlov, in which an existing involuntary reflex response is associated with a new stimulus. The new stimulus is presented at the same time as another stimulus that already produces the response. After the two have been presented together a number of times, the new stimulus produces the same response, even in the absence of the original stimulus.
Cognitive Approach	The cognitive approach uses experimental research methods to study internal mental processes such as attention, perception, memory and decision-making. Cognitive psychologists assume that the mind actively processes information from our senses (touch, taste etc.) and that between stimulus and response is a series of complex mental processes, which can be studied scientifically. They also assume that humans can be viewed as data processing systems and that the workings of a computer and the human mind are alike – they encode and store information, they have outputs, etc.
Comparison of Approaches	Comparison of approaches involves identifying similarities and differences between the different approaches in psychology. They can be compared in terms of criteria such as the different issues and debates (e.g. determinism, reductionism, nature versus nurture).
Congruence	Congruence is a term used by Carl Rogers (a humanistic psychologist) to describe a state in which a person's ideal self and actual experience are consistent or very similar. However, Rogers felt that it was rare for a complete state of congruence to exist and that all people experience a certain amount of incongruence.
Counselling Psychology	Counselling psychology focuses on providing therapeutic treatments to clients who experience a wide variety of symptoms, to help people of all ages deal with emotional, social, developmental, and other life concerns. Humanistic psychology has provided several approaches to counselling and therapy. For example, person-centered therapy was developed by Carl Rogers. This is non-directive and the client is encouraged to discover their own solutions within a warm, supportive and non-judgemental environment.
Defence Mechanisms	Defence mechanisms are unconscious strategies used by the ego to manage anxiety by redirecting psychic energy. Examples include repression (burying an unpleasant thought or desire in the unconscious) and displacement (where emotions are directed away from their source or target, towards other things).
Denial	Denial is a defence mechanism where a threatening thought is ignored or treated as if it were not true. For example, a wife might find evidence that her husband is cheating on her, but dismiss it and provide other reasons/explanation for her husband's behaviour.
Displacement	Displacement is a defense mechanism where emotions are directed away from their source or target, towards something else. For example, a boss gives his employee a hard time at work and the employee goes home and shouts at this wife.
Ego	According to Sigmund Freud's tripartite theory of personality, the ego is the part of personality that acts rationally, balancing the id and the superego. It develops at 2-4 years old and acts according to the 'reality principle'.

Emergence of Cognitive Neuroscience	Cognitive neuroscience is an academic field that studies the influence of brain structures on mental processes. The emergence of cognitive neuroscience occurred due to advances in brain imaging techniques such as fMRI and PET scans, which allow scientists to study the neurobiological basis of mental processes like memory.
Emergence of Psychology as a Science	The psychology emerged as a science at the beginning of the 20th Century when the early behaviourists began to question the scientific status and value of introspection. John Watson argued that rather than focus on subjective 'private' mental processes, psychology should study objective phenomena that could be observed and measured. This was the starting point for both the behaviourist approach and psychology emerging as a scientific discipline.
Evolution	Evolution refers to gradual changes in an inherited characteristic of a species over many generations. Darwin explained this in terms of 'survival of the fittest' (i.e. the best adapted to the local environment), meaning that any characteristic or behaviour that increases the chance that an individual will survive and reproduce, would be passed onto future generations.
Focus on the Self	Humanistic ideas about behaviour often focus on the self, which is an individual's consciousness in relation to their own identity. Carl Rogers believed that people could only fulfil their potential for personal growth if they had positive self-regard.
Free Will	Humanistic psychologists believe that humans have free will. Humans are able to make their own decisions and are not determined by biological or environmental factors.
Genes	Genes are the biochemical units of heredity that make up chromosomes. Genes are segments of DNA molecules that code physical features (e.g. eye colour) and psychological features (e.g. intelligence).
Genetic Basis of Behaviour	The genetic basis of behaviour refers to the idea that genes can be responsible for behaviour (e.g. attachment), as well as for physical characteristics (e.g. eye colour). The genotype refers to the inherited genetic materials, whereas the phenotype is the expression of a person's genotype, produced by interaction of the genotype and the environment.
Genotype	The genotype is a person's unique genetic make-up that is coded in their chromosomes and fixed at conception. However, the expression of a genotype is influenced by environmental factors and becomes a person's phenotype.
Humanistic Psychology	Humanistic psychology is an approach that emphasises the study of the whole person and sees people as being active in their own development. It is a person-centred approach, which views every individual as unique and regards personal growth and fulfilment in life as a basic human motive.
Id	According to Sigmund Freud's tripartite theory of personality, the id is the part of personality that exists from birth and drives us. According to Freud, the id acts according to the 'pleasure principle'.
Identification: SLT	Identification involves internalising and adopting behaviours shown by a role model, because they have a quality the individual would like to possess. For example, they might be attractive or of high status.
Imitation	Imitation is a term used by social learning theorists to describe the way in which an individual copies the behaviour of a role model.
Inferences	Inferences are conclusions reached on the basis of evidence and reasoning. Cognitive psychologists use computer models to draw conclusions (make inferences) regarding mental processes.
Internal Mental Processes	According to the Cognitive Approach, internal mental processes are operations that occur in the mind, but can be studied scientifically. They are also known as mediational processes because they occur between the stimulus and the response. Examples include memory, attention and perception.
Introspection	Introspection refers to observing and examining your own conscious thoughts and emotions. Wundt first used this method in the earliest psychology laboratory, set up in Germany in 1879,
Maslow's Hierarchy of Needs	Maslow's hierarchy of needs is a theory of human motivation. The needs are presented in a five-level sequence, where basic needs (e.g. for food and shelter) have to be met before higher psychological needs (e.g. for esteem and self-actualisation).
Modelling: SLT	Modelling is a process that occurs during Social Learning. Modelling can occur when an observer imitates a role model, or when a person produces a specific behaviour (acting as a model) that may then be imitated.
Neurochemistry	Neurochemistry in the context of the biological approach refers to the chemical processes occurring in the nervous system. For example, the actions of neurotransmitters within the brain.

Operant Conditioning	Operant conditioning is a type of learning investigated by Skinner, in which a new voluntary behaviour is associated with a consequence. Reinforcement (positive or negative) makes the behaviour more likely to occur, whereas punishment makes it less likely to occur.
Pavlov	Ivan Pavlov was a Russian biologist who first demonstrated classical conditioning. He was able to show that dogs could learn to salivate to a bell or a buzzer, if it was paired with food.
Phenotype	The phenotype is the expression of a person's genetic make-up (genotype) that can be influenced by the environment.
Psychodynamic Approach	The psychodynamic approach is often associated with Sigmund Freud, who theorised that our mental activity is mostly unconscious, and that this unconscious activity shapes our behaviour. He explained that traumatic childhood experiences can lead to psychological disorders, and developed 'talking cures' (psychoanalysis, more generally termed psychotherapy) to help release problematic repressed memories and relieve symptoms.
Psychosexual Stages	Freud believed that humans progress through 'psychosexual stages', during the development of the psyche. He named five stages, each with a particular characteristic behaviour: oral behaviour (0-18 months); anal – holding or discarding faeces (18 months – 3.5 years); phallic – fixation on genitals (3.5 – 6 years); latency – repressed sexual urges (6 years - puberty); and genital – awakened sexual urges (puberty onwards). Freud claimed that, during development, a child could become fixated on one of these stages, which could lead to specific psychological disorders.
Repression	Repression is a defence mechanism, which involves burying an unpleasant thought or desire in the unconscious (e.g. traumatic childhood experiences may be repressed and so forgotten).
Role of Conditions of Worth	Humanistic psychologists focus on the role of conditions of worth in explaining behaviour. People very often believe that they will only be loved and valued if they meet certain conditions of worth (e.g. being good, passing exams). These conditions of worth can create incongruity between the real self (how the person is) and the ideal self (how they think they should be). The person is motivated to close the gap between the real and ideal self but may do this in ways that make them unhappy. For example, they may choose a career or university course to make their parents happy.
Schemas	Schemas are cognitive frameworks that help us to organise and interpret information. They are developed through experience and can affect our cognitive processing.
Self-Actualisation	Self-actualisation is the final level or stage of Maslow's hierarchy of needs. Maslow found that individuals who attained this level share certain characteristics. These individuals are typically creative and have an accurate perception of themselves and the world around them.
Skinner	Skinner developed the theory of Operant Conditioning and first introduced the term 'reinforcement' to explain how the consequences of a particular behaviour can make future behaviours more or less likely.
Social Learning Theory: Approaches	The social learning theory is concerned with how people learn when they observe and imitate others. It can be seen as a bridge between the Behaviourist Approach and the Cognitive Approach as like the Behaviourist Approach, it emphasises the importance of environment and reinforcement in learning. However, like the Cognitive Approach, it acknowledges the important role that internal mental processes play in interpreting the environment and planning new actions.
Superego	According to Sigmund Freud's tripartite theory of personality, the superego is the part of personality concerned with keeping to moral norms. It develops around 4-5 years old and acts according to the 'morality principle', attempting to control a powerful id with feelings of guilt.
Mediational Processes	Mediational processes are mental (cognitive) factors that intervene in the learning process to determine whether a new behaviour is acquired or not. The four mediational processes proposed by Bandura are attention (whether we notice the behaviour); retention (whether we remember the behaviour); reproduction (whether we are able to perform the behaviour); and motivation (whether the perceived rewards outweigh the perceived costs).
Theoretical & Computer Models	Theoretical and computer models are used by cognitive psychologists to study mental processes. Theoretical models are diagrammatic representations of the steps involved in internal mental processes, e.g. the information-processing model. Computer models are software simulations of internal mental processes that are created in collaboration with computer scientists.

Reinforcement: SLT	According to Social Learning Theory, reinforcement can be direct or indirect. Direct reinforcement occurs when you perform a certain behaviour and are rewarded (positive reinforcement), or it leads to the removal or avoidance of something unpleasant (negative reinforcement). Indirect reinforcement occurs when you observe someone else perform a certain behaviour and receive either positive or negative reinforcement.
Unconscious	The unconscious mind consists of mental processes that are inaccessible to consciousness but still influence us. Freud believed that the unconscious mind was the primary source of human behaviour and stated that like an iceberg, the most important part of the mind is the part you cannot see (beneath the surface of the water/consciousness).
Vicarious Reinforcement	Vicarious reinforcement occurs when learners observe role models receiving either positive or negative reinforcement. This means that because the learner has observed the consequences of the behaviour they are more (or less) likely to imitate it, depending on what those consequences were.
Wundt	William Wundt opened the first psychology laboratory in Germany in 1879 and used it to study the human mind, using a technique known as introspection.

NOTES

NOTES

CHECKLIST

Specification	Content	
Origins of psychology	Origins of psychology: Wundt, introspection and the emergence of psychology as a science.	☐
Learning approaches	Classical and operant conditioning. Pavlov and Skinner's research. SLT including imitation, identification, modelling, vicarious reinforcement, the role of mediational processes and Bandura's research.	☐
Cognitive approach	Classical and operant conditioning, including Pavlov and Skinner's research. SLT including imitation, identification, modelling, vicarious reinforcement, the role of mediational processes and Bandura's research.	☐
Biological approach	The influence of genes, biological structures and neurochemistry on behaviour. Genotype and phenotype, genetic basis of behaviour, evolution and behaviour.	☐
Psychodynamic approach	The role of the unconscious, the structure of personality, that is ID, ego and superego, defence mechanisms including repression, denial and displacement, psychosexual stages.	☐
Humanistic psychology	Free will, self-actualisation and Maslow's hierarchy of needs, focus on the self, congruence, the role of conditions of worth. The influence on counselling psychology.	☐
Comparison of approaches	Comparison of approaches.	☐

www.tutor2u.net/psychology

AQA | A Level | Psychology

SKU: 03-4130-30180-03 | ISBN: 978-1915417251

AQA A LEVEL PSYCHOLOGY

tutor2u

EXAM BUSTER

Approaches in Psychology

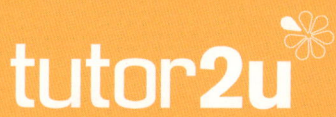

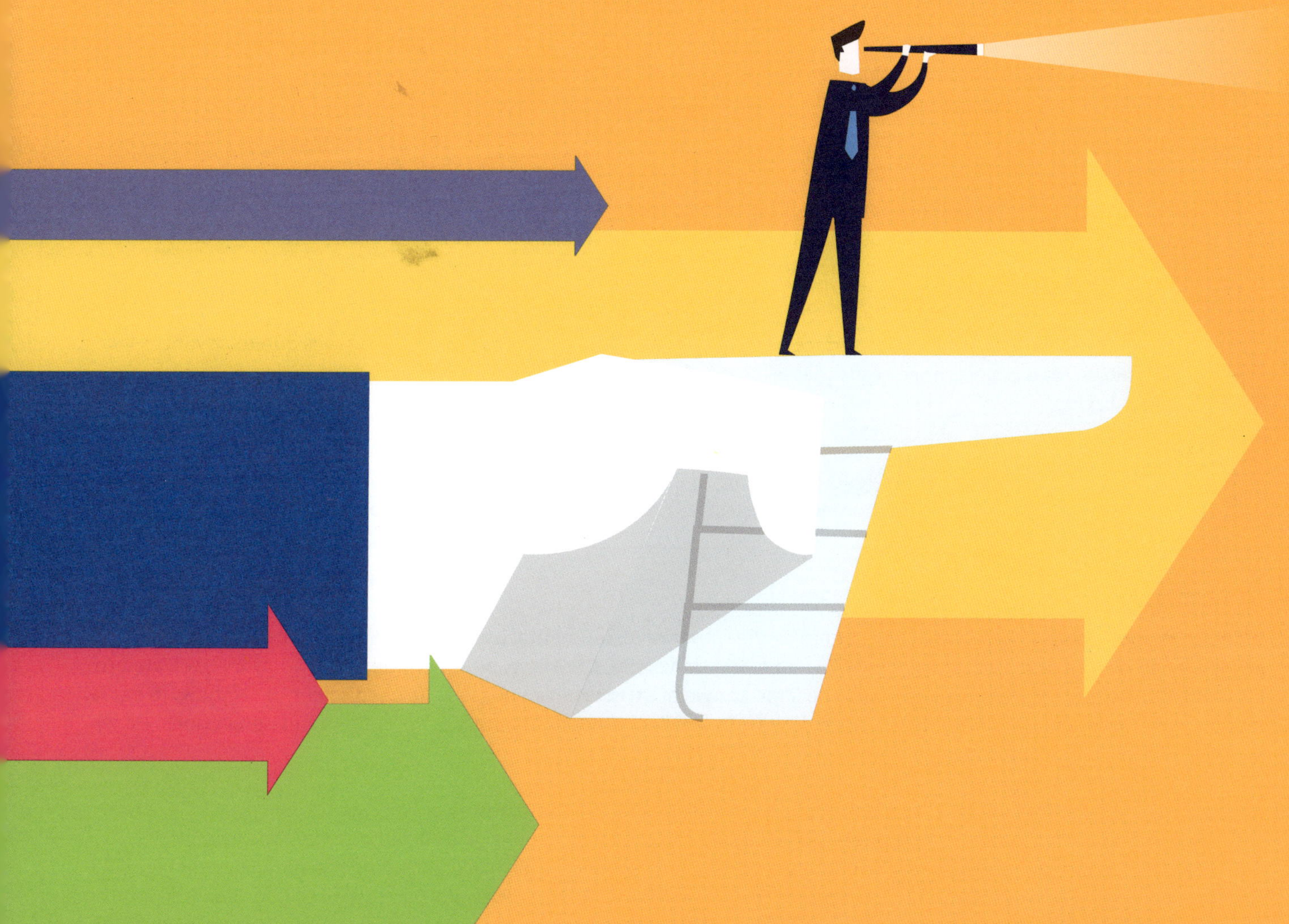

JOSEPH SPARKS & HELEN LAKIN

THE ORIGINS OF PSYCHOLOGY

Specification: Origins of psychology: Wundt, introspection and the emergence of psychology as a science.

WHAT YOU NEED TO KNOW
▪   Outline the origins of psychology, including the significance of Wilhelm Wundt and introspection.
▪   Outline the emergence of Psychology as a Science.

The Origins of Psychology

It is useful to understand the origins of psychology, by appreciating the emergence of different psychological approaches over time. The timeline below outlines the origins of psychology from Wilhelm Wundt in 1879, to the emergence of cognitive neuroscience in 2000.

1879	**Wundt** opened the first experimental psychology laboratory in Leipzig, Germany and, as a result, Psychology began to emerge as its own discipline. Before this, in the 17-19th centuries, psychology only was regarded as an experimental branch within philosophy.
1900	**Freud** established the **psychodynamic approach**. He highlighted the importance of the unconscious mind on behaviour and developed his own therapy called **psychoanalysis.**
1913	**Watson** and **Skinner** established the **behaviourist approach**. They criticised Freud and Wundt, arguing that true scientific psychology should restrict itself to studying phenomena that can be directly observed and measured. They believed that *all* behaviour is learnt and that psychologists should only be interested in observable behaviours.
The 1950s	**Rogers** and **Maslow** developed the **humanistic approach**. They rejected the views put forward by both the behaviourist and psychodynamic approaches and emphasised the importance of free will by attempting to understand the whole person.
The 1960s	Ten years later, the **cognitive approach** emerged with the introduction of the computer. The cognitive approach was interested in studying mental processes; cognitive psychologists believe that we can make inferences about how the mind works based on results from laboratory experiments.
The 1980s	The **biological approach** began to surface as the dominant approach in psychology. This was due to advances in technology, for example, brain scans that allow psychologists to have an increased understanding of the functioning human brain.
2000	Most recently, cognitive neuroscience has emerged in the forefront of psychology, which brings together the biological and cognitive approaches. This approach investigates how biological structures influence mental states.

Wundt and Introspection

Wilhelm Wundt (1832-1920) is often considered as the father of experimental psychology and was the first person to acknowledge himself as a psychologist. In 1875, at Leipzig University, Germany, he set up the first laboratory dedicated to experimental psychology. Wundt's approach became known as **structuralism** because he used scientific methods to study human consciousness by breaking its structure down into smaller components, such as sensations and perceptions. He developed a technique, known as introspection.

Introspection means "looking into" and is the process in which a person examines their inner world, by consciously observing their thoughts and emotions. Wundt trained his participants so that they could give detailed observations from their introspection. He strictly controlled the environment where introspection took place, including the stimuli (e.g. images or sounds) and tasks (e.g. a description of their perception or emotions) that participants were asked to consider. The information Wundt gleaned from his participants' introspection was used to shed light on the processes involved in human consciousness.